GULF OF MEXICO

Rio Tempisque Basin

SIERRA MADRE

Isla del Tiburon
Obregon Marshes
Laguna Agiambampo
Bahia de Topolobampo
Ensenada del Pabellon
Marismas nacionales
San Blas

Imperial Valley

Gulf of California

Bahia San Quintin
Laguna Scammon
Laguna San Ignacio
Bahia Magdalena

PACIFIC OCEAN

TRACKS IN THE SKY

WILDLIFE AND WETLANDS OF THE PACIFIC FLYWAY

PHOTOGRAPHS BY TUPPER ANSEL BLAKE

TEXT BY PETER STEINHART

CHRONICLE BOOKS · SAN FRANCISCO

PUBLISHED IN ASSOCIATION WITH THE NATIONAL AUDUBON SOCIETY

Copyright © 1987 by Tupper Ansel Blake
and Peter Steinhart. All rights reserved.
No part of this book may
be reproduced in any form without written
permission from the publisher.

Printed in Japan by Dai Nippon Printing Co., Ltd., Tokyo

Library of Congress Cataloging in Publication Data

Blake, Tupper Ansel.
  Tracks in the sky.

  Includes index.
  1. Wetland ecology—West (U.S.) 2. Wetland
conservation—West (U.S.) 3. Birds—West (U.S.)—
Ecology. 4. Birds—West (U.S.)—Migration. 5. Zoology
—West (U.S.) 6. Wetlands—West (U.S.) I. Steinhart,
Peter. II. Title. III. Title: Pacific flyway.
QL155.B55 1987   598.2′52632′0979   87-9379
ISBN 0−87701−351−9

Editing: Terry Ryan
Composition: G & S Typesetters

Distributed in Canada by
Raincoast Books
112 East 3rd Avenue
Vancouver, B.C.
V5T 1C8

10 9 8 7 6 5 4 3 2 1

The publication of this book was made possible in part by the
generous assistance of the National Audubon Society.

A selection of the photos from this book also appears in *Tracks in
the Sky,* an exhibition organized by the California Academy of
Sciences and circulated by the Smithsonian Institution Traveling
Exhibition Service.

Chronicle Books
San Francisco, California

CONTENTS

FOREWORD

When President Theodore Roosevelt issued an executive order "reserving and setting apart . . . Pelican Island as a preserve and breeding ground for native birds," few people realized the magnitude of this action. But on that day in March 1903, the National Wildlife Refuge System was born. Roosevelt not only created the system, he gave it momentum and direction.

During his tenure, Teddy Roosevelt created a total of fifty-three units of the National Wildlife Refuge System in seventeen states and territories. In one day alone in February 1909, the president created seventeen refuges by executive order. These areas set aside for wildlife were not insignificant pieces of rock or ice. On the contrary, some of the most superlative wildlife spectacles in the world were preserved when Roosevelt acted. In the Pacific flyway, the immense wetlands of the Yukon Delta in Alaska, the Malheur country in Oregon, and the Klamath Basin in northeastern California all owe their existence to Roosevelt's vision.

Not everyone immediately grasped Roosevelt's vision of protecting wildlife by reserving large habitat areas. Congress, for one, didn't jump on the bandwagon. In fact, since the president had bypassed legislative channels in creating the refuges, Congress refused to appropriate funds to operate and guard the refuges for over thirty years.

At about the same time that Roosevelt issued the executive order preserving Pelican Island, the National Audubon Society was fledging. Formed by sportsmen and conservationists concerned with the senseless slaughter of birds and wildlife that occurred in the latter 19th century, the society already had a long-standing relationship with Roosevelt when he became president.

So when Roosevelt needed guards to protect the newly created National Wildlife Refuges, Audubon wardens did the job. By 1910 when Roosevelt left office, Audubon had forty-four wardens to protect bird populations and nesting colonies across the country. Audubon wardens uncovered market hunting (hunting for profit) at Tule and Eagle lakes that totally decimated the western grebe colonies there. Twelve market hunters had collected $30,000 for grebe skins at markets in San Francisco—a more lucrative occupation than robbing banks. An Audubon warden on the Klamath refuge arrested the mayor and three prominent citizens from a nearby town for killing ducks illegally. In the southeast, three Audubon wardens were killed protecting wildlife during this period.

Not all of Audubon's work for Pacific flyway wetlands and wetland-associated wildlife occurred in the western U.S. Through the efforts of Audubon and its president, T. Gilbert Pearson, in 1916, the U.S. signed the Migratory Bird Treaty with Canada. This treaty had been vigorously opposed by states' rights advocates until Pearson included a "dicky bird" amendment in the legislation. With this amendment protecting migratory songbirds attached to the bill, support grew quickly. Once passed and signed, the treaty ended spring shooting, prohibited all shorebird hunting, and established bag and season limits on waterfowl.

Much has been accomplished in the ensuing years in the area of habitat protection by reserving land for wildlife and by managing wildlife through education and regulations based on the Migratory Bird Treaty. Unfortunately, but not surprisingly, much remains to be done if we are to secure a future that includes shorebirds scooting along a mud flat and a long V of geese flying into an autumn sunset.

The pressures on the remaining natural lands as a place where organisms can make a living will continue to grow as our western human population increases. The following statistic is telling: 60 percent of the migratory birds of the Pacific flyway winter in California's Central Valley, where only 5 percent of the historic wetland habitat remains. The goal is clear—not only must we protect what's left of these wetlands on which so much wildlife depends, we must restore former wetlands and reestablish their viability for wildlife.

The importance of this book is the opportunity it represents to educate and inform the citizenry of the values and beauty in our western wetlands. We hope this book will be a call to commitment to conserve these incredible areas. I'm optimistic because, though a person of Teddy Roosevelt's vision and standing may come along only once or twice in a nation's life, we have, as this book accurately describes, the hope of the Mike Houcks, Lynn Tennefosses, John Cowans, and Steve Hermans carrying our stewardship responsibility into the future.

One can already feel the momentum building as conservationists, hunters, and birdwatchers alike unite into a positive force advocating a quality of life in the west that includes cranes, swans, ducks, geese, and shorebirds for all of us. The right investment now will pay dividends to our children's children by allowing them to be molded and mesmerized by our rich natural heritage, just as we were. For that reason, Audubon is proud to sponsor this book.

Glenn Olson
National Audubon Society

ACKNOWLEDGEMENTS

I wish you good luck in finding your way about the wetlands of western North America—camera in hand." Those words of encouragement were written to me by my friend A. Starker Leopold in January 1983. Little did I realize that this new venture we were collaborating on—a photographic survey of the Pacific flyway—would absorb roughly five years of my life, take me from the tundra to the tropics, and provide a wildlife photographer with the opportunity of a lifetime. Starker advised and guided me in the development of this project. I shall forever be indebted to him.

The initial support and funding for the fieldwork was provided by several individuals and foundations. To Sherman Chickering, who believed in the project from the outset, I extend my deepest appreciation. I wish to express my gratitude also to the following, among others: the Weiler Foundation; the Sorensen Foundation; the Dean Witter Foundation; Peter Seligmann of the Nature Conservancy; the S. D. Bechtel, Jr., Foundation; Ned Spieker; the Irvine Foundation; the Gamble Foundation; the Marshall Steel Foundation; and the California Waterfowl Association. When the fieldwork required an extension, additional support and funding was given by many of the foregoing, as well as by Rusty Hale, Peter Stent, Peter Applegate, Peter McCuen, and Chris Steele.

In moving about and photographing along the Pacific flyway, I received the help and cooperation of many people who gave freely of their valuable time and advice. In particular I am grateful to: James Bartonek, Pacific Flyway Representative, U.S. Fish and Wildlife Service; Dirk Derksen and Margaret Petersen, U.S. Fish and Wildlife Service, Alaska; Pete and Belle Mickelson, Cordova, Alaska; Dennis Raveling, University of California at Davis; Tom Barry and Ernie Kuyt, Canadian Wildlife Service; Jose "Pity" Salomon, Antonio Encinas, and Juan Guzman of Mexico; Jim Lewis and Gary Stiles of Costa Rica.

In thanking folks, I would be remiss if I didn't pay tribute to the bush planes and their pilots, who throughout the far north of Alaska and Canada, as well as remote sections of Mexico and Costa Rica, landed me on water and snow, sand and grass. My sincere thanks are due to Bruce Conant, Jack Hodges, Bill Butler, and Rod King, pilot/biologists with the U.S. Fish and Wildlife Service, Alaska. Across the line in Canada, I thank Don Twitty, Ft. Chipewyan, Alberta; Freddie Carmichael of Inuvik, N.W.T.; and Willy Laserich and Ian Blewett of Cambridge Bay, N.W.T. For the aerial work in Mexico, I am much obliged to Jim Stewartt and David Caswell. Be it with floats, skis, or wheels, these small planes and their pilots' skills allowed me to see and photograph the isolated locations of the Pacific flyway.

To those people living off the wetlands, I owe a special thank you. To the Yupik eskimo of western Alaska, catching and drying their salmon. To the Inupiat eskimo boys at Pt. Barrow, dividing their time between hunting eider ducks and wrestling—between manhood and childhood. To Rosy and Freddie Albert, Elijah Allen and family, and the other Inuvialuit eskimo of the Mackenzie Delta, who took us into their whaling camps and into their hearts, giving hospitality, tea, and lore. To Louis Marten, John "Scarface" Marten and wife—Cree Indians of the Peace-Athabasca Delta—who shared their fish camps, and to the younger Crees who were off hunting moose. To the oystermen of Willapa Bay and the herring fishermen of Tomales and San Francisco Bays, who bring protein to the tables of the modern world. To the nameless but not faceless shrimpers of Mexico, be they offshore in large boats or plying the estuaries in dug out log canoes. To those vaqueros of coastal Costa Rica, who know the ways of wildlife but have never seen a field guide. You all taught me a great deal.

Traveling by bush planes, whaleboats, canoes, airboats, and on foot, I spent three years out on the wetlands of western North America gathering this collection of images. I take this opportunity to thank Marty Cappelletti of the Smithsonian Institution Traveling Exhibition Service for coordinating the results and putting all of this work into an exhibition for the Smithsonian Institution. I extend heartfelt thanks to Bob Kosturak, Madeleine Graham, and Joyce Gilio at the California Academy of Sciences, which worked with the Smithsonian Institution to mount an exhibition for a national tour. I also want to express my appreciation to the state historical societies of California, Oregon, and Washington, as well as to the Bancroft Library and the Lowie Museum of Anthropology, both in Berkeley, California, and to the Hudson's Bay Company, Winnipeg, Manitoba, for assistance in locating historical photographs and artifacts.

To allow the natural progression to move from photographic survey to exhibition to book, I am grateful to *San Francisco Chronicle* Publisher Dick Thieriot and Assistant Publisher Phelps Dewey, and to all their staff at Chronicle Books. Special mention must be given to the eye of book designer Steve Renick. Thanks also to Glenn Olson of the National Audubon Society for his support.

I am honored to team up with my friend and the author of this book, Peter Steinhart, a writer who devotes such time and skill to the task before him. His curiosity, insight, and love of the subject matter have created a book that images alone would not equal. The pleasure has been all mine.

On those occasions when the location was too remote or the situation too dangerous to go solo, I enlisted the assistance of Mike Whitt and Bob Fisher, who helped with carrying equipment, bringing food and fresh drinking water, and locating wildlife. The memories of the beautiful country and wildlife spectacles along the Pacific flyway will always burn brighter in my mind because of the many campfires I shared with these two fine compañeros.

In closing, I thank everyone—mentioned here or not—who played a part in the Pacific flyway story, whether through fundraising, fieldwork, museum exhibition, or the preparation of this book. Your trust and patience was greatly appreciated.

Tupper Ansel Blake
Inverness, California

The author wishes to thank the following people for giving generously of their time, experience, insight, and hospitality. Dirk Derksen, U.S. Fish and Wildlife Service, Anchorage, Alaska; Mat Bean, Association of Village Council Presidents, Bethel, Alaska; Ron Perry and the staff of the Yukon Delta National Wildlife Refuge, Bethel, Alaska; Jim and Mary Lou King, Juneau, Alaska; Ed Hoffman, Alberta Fish and Wildlife Division, Brooks, Alberta; Jay Bartsch, Ducks Unlimited, Brooks, Alberta; Jack Davis, Olympia, Washington; Jim Bartonek, U.S. Fish and Wildlife Service, Portland, Oregon; Mike Houck, Portland Audubon Society, Portland, Oregon; David Lockman, Wyoming Department of Game and Fish; John Cowan, Gridley, California; Mickey Heitmeier, University of California at Davis; Gary Zahm, San Luis National Wildlife Refuge, Los Banos, California; Paul Kelly, California Department of Fish and Game; and Lynn Tennefoss, Santa Clara Valley Audubon Society, Palo Alto, California. Without their efforts and the efforts of others like them, there would soon be no Pacific Flyway.

Peter Steinhart

Just west of Hoquiam on the Washington coast, there is a newly discovered spectacle. Tucked into an embayment of Grays Harbor, between the Hoquiam airstrip and the somber green cliffs of the forested shoreline, is a tide flat that receives the high tides late and slips them quickly back to sea, and so attracts most of the shorebirds of Grays Harbor. For five or six days in April, the tide flat draws sandpipers and dowitchers in increasing numbers. As you walk out along the wet meadow by the airstrip, you see birdwatchers traipsing back from the point in gum boots and parkas. They are, to a person, starry-eyed, shaking their heads as if to hear the wonder rattle.

What they have seen is something strange, wonderful, and beautiful. Crowded onto the tide flats in the 1,700-acre Bowerman Basin are 350,000 shorebirds. Tiny western sandpipers, long-billed dowitchers, and dunlins scurry like feathered crabs, belly to belly with their own reflections in the wet mud. They are feeding on a species of amphipod that breeds in stunning numbers in the mud. The sandpipers are bright buff and cinnamon in their spring plumage. They have flown here in ribbons and streamers of thirty or forty birds, wheeling and darting over tide flats and salt marshes all the way from Peru and Mexico. They have hardly been noticed by humans in these small bands. But here, they command attention.

Traditionally, the sandpipers have clustered here each April. They will stay only a few days and then, almost en masse, rise off the tide flats, head out to sea, and make a nonstop 1,500-mile flight to Alaska's Copper River Delta. It is as if they had come here to celebrate the annual tilting of the earth and the arrival of spring. While gathered in this enormous flock, they fly up from the mud flats, wheel as a group, and return to earth. As they turn, the white of their underwings flashes brightly. They form huge spirals of brown and black, then burst like an exploding star in dazzling white, then roll again like a vast muddy wave over the tide flats. The sight is shimmering, ephemeral, spectacular.

On a sunny April afternoon, as a high tide crowds the birds up to the edge of the flats, Steve Herman, a biologist from Evergreen College, has gathered his ornithology class at the edge of the water. In wire-rimmed sunglasses and an army surplus field jacket, Herman looks more like an aging hippie than a birdwatcher. But there is nothing slack-jawed or misty-eyed about him. He is as focused and intent as a fox in a poultry yard. He and the students have estimated that there are 350,000 shorebirds clustered on perhaps eight acres of mud flat. There are, they guess, more birds hiding from the wind in the sedge and grass at the upper edge of the basin. Right now, perhaps 45 percent of the shorebirds in the ninety-four square miles of Grays Harbor are concentrated in an area not much larger than a city block.

And they are performing what appears to be a dance. They rise and fall, catching the spring sunlight in the white of their wings and throwing it back at the sky. The feathering of half a million wings gusts like distant applause. It is not a celebration. A young peregrine falcon has swooped down into the flock, hoping to drive a panicky sandpiper out, and the sandpipers have been launched into the air by the danger. Alone, a sandpiper is an easy mark for a falcon. In this vast flock, the hunt is not so easy. "Westerns will fly straight at him," says Herman, "and he can't catch anything. You can see the value of the flock." The sandpipers move at perhaps forty miles per hour straight at the peregrine, which is doing eighty. At that speed and proximity, the sandpipers must simply dissolve at the outer edges of the falcon's vision before he can get a fix on one.

Herman, binoculars pressed against his bottle-cap sunglasses, barks out a narration of what the peregrine is doing. "He's up. Over the clear-cut. Now, just breaking the skyline. To the left of the shorebirds. There he goes. Nice stoop! Now he's up again." The shorebirds, as if in cadence to Herman's directions, rise and swirl, tumble like a breaking wave, dodging the peregrine as it sweeps through the flock. It disappears into the cloud of birds as if into a tunnel, and comes out the other side empty-taloned. Behind it the shorebirds still wheel and spiral. "It's like a movie!" exclaims Herman. "Look at that roll! I just love it! A river of birds!"

For four days, this gathering at Bowerman will go on. It is the largest concentration of shorebirds on spring migration on the Pacific coast south of Alaska.

King eiders, Pt. Barrow, Alaska

Perhaps the strangest thing about it is that Bowerman Basin became known to birdwatchers and scientists only six years ago. The Port of Grays Harbor intended to fill the basin and lease the newly created land to industry. Herman and University of Washington biologist Dave Paulson had begun to look at the area because they knew that it supported endangered peregrine falcons and that filling the basin would threaten them. Herman happened to come to Bowerman Basin looking for peregrines on the right day in April and stumbled onto the thousands of shorebirds. He discounts his role as a discoverer. "There were a lot of local people who knew it was around," he says. "We started counting the shorebirds here in 1981. It was known locally back in the 1920s and 1930s. I talked to an old guy who was upset about us paying so much attention to so few birds. He said when he was a small boy, there were *really* lots of 'em."

Port development threatened the basin until Herman presented a study to the U.S. Army Corps of Engineers documenting the high shorebird populations. He drew birdwatchers and Environmental Protection Agency (EPA) officials to the basin to show them what he had found. EPA officials decided to oppose the port's plans for filling. Herman feels, "It was not the scientific stuff or the endangered species that sold this place. The thing that turned the tide was the beauty."

In part, it was the beauty of vast numbers of self-willed, purposeful, independent creatures, lending the magnificence of their impulse to our sometimes drab, stay-at-home existence. We are fascinated with masses of living things—with the great herds of bison that roamed the west or the teeming migration of wildebeest flowing over the African plains. Early Californians marveled at the Sacramento Valley, where ducks and geese spread over ponds and grasslands as far as the eye could see. Today, we feel the same amazement when 200,000 snow geese cluster on California's Klamath Basin in November, or when 100,000 phalaropes dazzle the desert sky over Mono Lake. Such sights suggest that the world is rich with possibility, aswarm with intelligence, will, and purpose.

It is also the beauty of migration, the wonder and symmetry of large numbers of creatures dropped onto our imaginations from the sky, dangled before our eyes for a few days, and then jerked out of sight

and sound. The arrival and departure of geese and sandpiper, swallow and eagle, open for us seams in the cosmos, pose for us the possibility of a dimension beyond our own reality, a destination we, our boots nailed to our floors, are powerless to leap into. The sound of migrating geese overhead came to poet Charles Roberts "with a sanction and an awe profound, a boding of unknown, foreshadowed things." Frederick Peterson saw in "the dark flying rune" of geese "the sweep and loneliness of things . . . symbols of autumns vanished long ago . . . symbols of coming springs." When Herman looks out over the thousands of clustered wills at Bowerman Basin, he thinks "of a time when the city has gone down, when man regains the dignity of room and the value of rareness."

There was a time when we were more attuned to the movements of this tide, a time when we lived more out of doors and less insulated by concrete and glass and the shrill whine of urban life. Farmers in the thirteenth century set aside special days for listening for the first cuckoo in spring. Naturalist John Bartram observed that Pennsylvania farmers looked for the first bird of passage each March as a sovereign sign that the danger of frost was past and that it was time to plant peas and beans. A few people today live enough out under skies to continue that tradition of looking up in spring. Ed Hoffman, a biologist with the Alberta Division of Fish and Wildlife, records the dates of the first arrivals every year. He reflects upon the bleakness and cold of the Canadian prairie in winter and feels that when he sees the first bird, "To me, that's the end of winter. It still gives me a thrill when I see the first goose."

Those who see migration are possessed by a desire to reach out and touch the tide, to let it run through their fingers, to let it cool and animate the imagination. It is much the kind of fascination we have with moving water, much the same impulse that makes us want to skip stones across a creek or wade into the surf at a beach. We want to lay hands upon it, to begin to encompass the reach and will and mystery of that tide as it passes us by. Some reach out by painting pictures of vast, watery, marshland skies, and ducks rising from the cattails, as if freezing the ever-changing sky and the wings of birds might bring the artist closer to the meaning of the journey. Gary Zahm, manager of the San Luis National Wildlife

Refuge in California, does it by stopping a hunter on the refuge to pinch the breast of a freshly killed pintail. He wants to see what kind of condition the bird is in, to gauge in the dime's thickness of fat expended the reach of a 1,500-mile flight from an Alberta pothole. Biologist Albert Hochbaum, who studied ducks at Canada's Delta Research Station, would go out on a November evening, when frost first spread over the marsh, and watch the spectacular departure, en masse, of hundreds of thousands of ducks. Duck hunters try to participate by learning the language of ducks. In Manitoba, some guides can, using only their voices, reproduce faithfully the sexual invitation of a mallard, the trilling call of a scaup, or the growl of a canvasback.

Migration is a mystery. Since most of the great migrating flocks move at night, we humans are only dimly aware of their passage. Often, we observe migration only when we have stuck a thumb into the air on some foggy night and accidentally brought down a passing starling. The collision stuns us. When the torch on the Statue of Liberty was lighted, maintenance crews picked up seven hundred dead birds a month at its base. One night, more than five thousand birds struck a radio tower in Georgia and lay dead on the ground the next morning. Fifty thousand were killed one night over Werner Robbins Air Force Base in Georgia, crashing into one another while circling the airfield's lights. A German lighthouse keeper early in this century wrote of a spring night: "The whole sky is now filled with a babel of hundreds of thousands of voices, and as we approach the lighthouse there presents itself to the eye a scene which more than confirms the experience of the ear. Under the intense glare of the light, swarms of larks, starlings, and thrushes careen around in ever-varying density, like showers of brilliant sparks or huge snowflakes driven onwards by a gale, and are continuously replaced as they disappear by freshly arriving multitudes."

The river of birds is huge and continuous. Herman's 350,000 sandpipers are but a tiny eddy in the current. Each fall, it moves like a falling veil over the north, as if some God had turned out a basketful of creatures and watched them tumble over the horizon. Each spring, birds move in wedges and ribbons, pairs and clusters, from lake to lake, skulking over the upland forests, leapfrogging along our coasts. They

Emperor geese, Yukon-Kuskokwim Delta, Alaska

are as much a part of the sky above us as the clouds and stars. And when they bump into our conscious minds, they startle us with the idea that there is life and will moving around outside us.

For most of our history, we have had to invent folklore to explain this phenomenon. Cicero said geese slept on their flights, one bird's head on the back of the bird in front of it. Aristotle told us that redstarts changed into robins and that swallows shed their feathers and went down rodent holes to hibernate in winter. Olaus Magnus told us that swallows wintered in great masses under the sea, "joined bill to bill, wing to wing, foot to foot." A British pamphlet in 1703 assured us that the birds flew to the moon for winter. Indians and Eskimos tell stories of small migrants hitching rides on the backs of sandhill cranes. The Irish believed that barnacle geese hatched from barnacles because the Gulf Stream brought ashore barnacle-crusted driftwood just before the geese arrived in winter.

It wasn't until humans began to travel widely and see the same birds in vastly different parts of the world that we began to understand migration. In the seventeenth century, naturalist John Ray read accounts of travelers and geographers and guessed that the swallows that disappeared in the fall were wintering in Egypt and Ethiopia. Understanding European migration patterns was complicated by the tendency of the birds to move from east to west, rather than from north to south across the Mediterranean. Those migrants that crossed the Mediterranean did so by night, so they could feed by day and rebuild the fat reserves lost in long flight. Daytime migrants moved southeast, crossed the Bosporus, and moved down the eastern shore of the Mediterranean into Africa. Bellonius reported kites crossing the Bosporus "in such great numbers, I dare confidently affirm they would exceed the numbers of men living on the earth." Some species make such complicated migrations that we still don't fully understand them. Wheatears that breed in Alaska cross China and India to winter in Africa. The red-footed falcon breeds in eastern China, crosses the Indian Ocean, and winters in South Africa.

Some birds migrate three times a year. Black brant, for example, fly from Mexico to Alaska's Yukon-Kuskokwim Delta to breed. Then they fly to specific lakes north of the Arctic Circle to molt. They stay flightless on these lakes for four or five weeks, then fly south to staging areas, such as Izembek Lagoon on the Alaska Peninsula, to fatten for the fall flight. Finally, they fly three thousand miles, nonstop, across the Pacific in forty-five to sixty hours to California or Mexico. King eider drakes leave their mates as the eggs of the year hatch on the Perry River and Mackenzie River deltas of the Arctic and fly west along the coast of the Beaufort Sea to molt in offshore rafts two hundred miles southwest of Point Lay in the Chukchi Sea. Then they fly south to winter in the Bering Sea and the Aleutians.

Migration routes in North America are more easily understood than migration routes in Europe, because the Rocky Mountains, the Mississippi River Valley, and the Appalachian Mountains divide the continent into discrete corridors running north and south. In 1952, Frederick C. Lincoln of the U.S. Bureau of the Biological Survey identified four separate flyways: the Pacific, the Central, the Mississippi, and the Atlantic. Many birds never cross the boundaries between these flyways. Many birds do. Snow geese breeding in the Arctic may fly down either the Pacific flyway or the Central flyway in the fall, and winter either in California or along the Texas Gulf coast. Ducks from the Alberta potholes may cross over to the Central flyway when they fly south in the fall. Swans breeding in Alaska have been found wintering on the Atlantic coast. No one yet knows whether these movements are genetically programmed, learned through tradition, or spurred by circumstance. Some patterns are rigid and precise. Analysis of the mineral content of the feathers of snow geese wintering in California show that nearly all of the geese wintering in the Sacramento National Wildlife Refuge were bred on Wrangel Island, while nearly all the geese fifteen miles away at Gray Lodge Waterfowl Management Area were bred on Banks Island. Some patterns aren't so rigid. Pintails bred in Alaska have gone all the way to Guatemala for winter. And sometimes there are travesties. On autumn days when a southwest wind pushes fog against the California coast, the tiny Farallon Islands, thirty miles west of San Francisco, may be the only land visible to migrants. Such days may bring to the Farallones an odd contingent of passengers. One October morning in 1984, the island's shrubs and rocks were crawling with errant migrants. Biologists there counted seventeen hundred exotics, including warblers from Massachusetts and the Great Lakes. On other days, researchers on the Farallones have found tropic birds from Tahiti and brown shrikes from Siberia.

It is the regularity of migration that is most astonishing. Bird banding, particularly by the U.S. Fish and Wildlife Service, has, since the 1920s, confirmed many of the patterns. Snow geese that winter in California nest on Wrangel Island in the Soviet Union. Pintails nesting in Alberta winter in California. Blue-winged teals from Alberta cross the equator to winter in Ecuador. Bristle-thighed curlews breed in Alaska and winter in Tahiti. Dusky Canada geese breed only on the Copper River Delta in Alaska and winter only in Oregon's Willamette Valley or the lower Columbia River. All the world's cackling Canada geese breed in Alaska's Yukon-Kuskokwim Delta and winter in California's Sacramento Valley. Some migrants fly as much as two thousand miles in a single flight to reach the precise wintering spot.

When you seek to discover how birds came to make such epic journeys and to bind themselves to specific places so far apart on the globe, you find that migration is especially a northern habit. Ninety-five percent of the landbirds that breed between forty and fifty degrees north latitude (roughly the area between San Francisco and Calgary or St. Louis and Winnipeg) migrate south for winter. There is little comparable migration among birds in the latitudes forty to fifty degrees south. The reason is that there is a vast amount of land forty or more degrees north of the equator but very little forty degrees or more south of it.

Migrants make use of similar habitat in summer and winter ranges. If they are forest-loving in summer, they are forest-loving in winter. Water birds in summer are water birds in winter because they are adapted to feeding on aquatic plants and animals. The reason many migrants make such long flights seems to be that the areas of similar character are spread out widely on the globe. There is, for example, little land comparable to California's Central Valley until you get to the Alberta potholes or Alaska's Copper River Delta. The Rocky Mountains veer over to the coast mountains north of Washington. In western Canada,

Stilt sandpiper, Kendall Island, Mackenzie Delta, N.W.T., Canada

the Ogilvies, the Mackenzies, the Wrangel and the Alaska ranges rumple the surface of the earth so that, between Oregon and Alaska, there is relatively little flat land. The birds that are married to marshy surroundings have a long way to go.

And most of the migrants—indeed, most of the birdlife of the world—depend upon permanent surface water. The blue-winged teal wintering along the coastal lagoons of Costa Rica need the potholes and marshes of northern latitudes in summer. There isn't sufficient wetland habitat in the tropics to support the greater territorial and nutritional needs of the birds during nesting season. Even the raptors and warblers, birds we don't usually think of as water-dependent, require the proximity of marshes and rivers. Golden eagles on the Sheldon National Wildlife Refuge in Nevada feed for much of the winter on Canada geese. Alaskan bald eagles are wedded to salmon runs, and they migrate into areas where warm water keeps salmon available in winter. Warblers and vireos may not be able to live far from streamside willows and alders.

The fact is, the great migrations are reflections in the sky of the waters of the globe. The Pacific flyway is but a corridor connecting the wetlands of the west. Wetlands are areas that are covered at some time of the day or the year by water, and so are wet enough to support aquatic plants and invertebrates. Wetlands may be tidal mud flats that are covered with water twice a day, or they may be desert playas that are flooded only a few days a year. They include the tidal zone along our rocky coasts and the courses of rivers that rise in flood season and subside in summer months.

It is the north's wetlands that bring the migrants. In winter, most of the north's water is locked away in ice and snow, and the birds must fly south. But in summer, the days are long, the ice melts, the ponds and sloughs become incredibly rich in aquatic life, and the birds return. North of forty-five degrees north latitude, huge amounts of the continent are wetlands. Sixty percent of Alaska is wetland. The vast river deltas of the Yukon, Kuskokwim, Copper, Mackenzie, Peace, and Athabaska all spread out enormous resources for water birds in summer. Ten percent of the lower forty-eight states were originally wetlands. The wide river valleys feeding into Puget

Sound, the vast marshland that was once California's Central Valley, the snowmelt from the Sierra Nevada and the Rocky Mountains that spills into great basin lakes all provided huge amounts of wetland habitat. And the migrants are wedded to these ponds and marshes and lakes and sloughs. Ornithologist Frank Bellrose observes that most waterfowl fly their migration routes over water and will turn to fly over large lakes. Ducks and geese flying southeast from Canadian prairie breeding grounds usually turn south as soon as they hit the Mississippi River. Cackling Canada geese migrating down the Pacific coast turn east at the Columbia River, follow it up to the Willamette, then follow the Willamette south before hopping over to the Klamath Basin.

So, that river of birds floats as much on water and mud as it drifts on wind and clouds. And, despite our sense of wonder about migration, we have been slow to see the links between sky and water. We have removed ourselves from the wetlands that host the migrants when they come down out of the air. Our rivers are encased in concrete, our swamps are drained, our tide flats are diked against the darker impulses of wind and moon. We have locked water away in pipes and taps, reservoirs, and flood-control channels. We want the landscape organized, dependably unchanging, solid and dry underfoot. America as a nation has pursued this desire with fervor. In a series of Swamp Acts, the federal government gave to the states much of the submerged and marshy lands, with the suggestion that the states drain and develop them. Draining swamps has been an act of patriotism and progressivism. And because of this, by 1977, the nation had drained approximately half of its original wetlands.

The remainder continues to decline. The U.S. Army Corps of Engineers processes eleven thousand applications a year to fill wetlands and rejects only 3 percent of them. The corps' jurisdiction extends to only 16 percent of the lands that are being drained; farmers who are not bound by the corps' regulations have been draining most of the rest to plant crops and so perhaps compensate for increased operating costs. We are still losing 500,000 acres of wetlands a year. Only 4 percent of the wetlands of California's Central Valley remain. Tidal flats in Louisiana are disappearing as flood-control works dump the Mississippi

River farther out to sea. Freshwater marshes in Minnesota are drained rapidly. Ninety-seven percent of the wetlands we lose are inland freshwater marshes, most of them unregulated by the Corps of Engineers. We are losing coastal marshes with almost equal speed.

Overseas the problem may be even more severe. As population increases, governments expect to meet food demands by reclaiming wetlands. "The potential for productive agriculture from these soils is incredible," says Orie Loucks of Butler University. "As world populations increase, we are going to go to clearing the wetlands to feed them." Already, Malaysia, Indonesia, and Jamaica have major clearing and colonization programs that have moved vast numbers of peasants into reclaimed wetlands. In Brazil, reclamation projects and dams to provide electricity have wrung out millions of acres of wetlands.

Wetlands all along the Pacific flyway are disappearing. We seem to be aware of the problem. A 1977 executive order called on federal agencies to try to do what they could to slow the pace of loss. Even Interior Secretary James Watt held that, "In contrast to other land purchases the Interior Department is authorized to make, we must move aggressively for wetland areas. They may not be available if we wait." But losses continue. Most wetlands are private lands, and state and federal agencies are reluctant to spend the money to buy them and even more reluctant to spend the money afterwards to manage them. Agencies charged with protecting wetlands are poorly funded. Agencies charged with regulating filling and dredging are not always committed to the task.

We seem powerless to stop the loss. And if we fail to provide for wetlands, we will dry up that river of birds. We will, in the process, do something to the human imagination. We will lose yet another source of wonder and hope and trust. We will lose yet another of our connections with the world outside ourselves, and draw further inward into a mood of doubt and timidity and greed. And that would be only part of our loss.

Emperor geese, Yukon-Kuskokwim Delta, Alaska

Ross' geese, Karrak Lake, Queen Maud Gulf, N.W.T., Canada

Arctic fox, Karrak Lake, Queen Maud Gulf, N.W.T., Canada

Belukha whale, Kendall Island, Mackenzie Delta, N.W.T., Canada

Yukon-Kuskokwim Delta, Alaska

Bar-tailed godwit, Yukon-Kuskokwim Delta, Alaska

Spectacled eiders, Yukon-Kuskokwim Delta, Alaska

Black brant, Yukon-Kuskokwim Delta, Alaska

Ogilvie Mountains, Yukon Territory, Canada

Oldsquaw, Yukon-Kuskokwim Delta, Alaska

Emperor goose gosling, Yukon-Kuskokwim Delta, Alaska

Beaufort Sea, Pt. Barrow, Alaska

Snow goose gosling, Kendall Island, Mackenzie Delta, N.W.T., Canada

Common eider, male, Yukon-Kuskokwim Delta, Alaska

Common eider, female, Yukon-Kuskokwim Delta, Alaska

Yukon-Kuskokwim Delta, Alaska

Cackling Canada geese, Yukon-Kuskokwim Delta, Alaska

Pacific white-fronted geese, Yukon-Kuskokwim Delta, Alaska

Red phalarope, Yukon-Kuskokwim Delta, Alaska

Alaska's Yukon-Kuskokwim Delta is a roadless area the size of Kentucky, 150 miles south of the Arctic Circle. It is a treeless expanse of winding slough and river and pond, sedge meadow, dwarf willow, and cottongrass, inhabited only by the Eskimos who live in fifty scattered villages. It is also one of the world's great wetlands and a breeding ground of astonishing richness. Vast runs of salmon come up the rivers in summer. The area hosts over 100 million birds. All the world's cackling Canada geese nest here. So do 90 percent of the emperor geese, virtually the entire Pacific population of white-fronted geese, all the black turnstones, most of the western sandpipers and tundra swans, and large numbers of spectacled eider, oldsquaw, and sandhill crane. Most of the snow geese that winter in California rest here on their way south from Wrangel Island. "I think without question it is the richest delta system in western North America," says Dirk Derkson, a U.S. Fish and Wildlife Service biologist in Anchorage.

Kokechik Bay, an icy lobe of the Bering Sea, is the edge of the delta. On a June day, the sedge meadows are still desert brown, the ponds and sloughs steely gray. The fog drifting in from the sea parts to give hints of blue, but the light is subdued and casts the scene in a monochromatic gray. There is life all around. On a spit of sedge-covered land, a dozen black brant have nested. They are small, ducklike geese, unusual in that they spend most of their lives on coastal salt water. All about them are peninsulas and islands on which cluster nesting brant, emperor geese, and eider ducks. Jaegers fly overhead and glaucous gulls stand around like street-corner toughs, waiting for a goose to leave its nest and expose the eggs. There are the cries of loons and oldsquaws. Unmated cackling geese fly by in groups of five or six, honking in hoarse voices. There are the shrill police-whistle cries of dunlin and the quiet mutterings of nesting brant. The sounds are strange and unmusical, voices at home with wind and ice and the fading edge of winter. All these creatures have come here to breed. For them, it is here that the Pacific flyway begins.

Brant nests are pillows of charcoal-gray down, as broad as dinner plates, as deep as teacups. When a brant leaves the nest, it pulls the down over the top of the eggs like a coverlet, and the down so insulates the eggs that they remain biscuit-warm for hours. Margaret Petersen, a young biologist working on her doctoral thesis, crouches over a nest, parts the down, and lifts an egg to her ear. She can hear the chick peeping within, scratching weakly with its egg tooth on the calcerous wall that stands between it and an enormous world.

Petersen has been studying the geese on this marsh for four years. She has watched them build their nests and lay their eggs, and she knows that exactly twenty-four days after the first brant egg is laid, it will hatch. Within a few hours, the others in the nest will hatch. Twenty-four hours later, the goslings will be on the water with their parents. All about them, sandpipers, dunlin, sandhill cranes, eiders, cacklers, emperor geese will be hatching and rearing their young. In succeeding days, the brant will walk across the marsh to Kokechik Bay to feed on the eelgrass. Brant are never found far from eelgrass, except perhaps on the molting lakes they visit at the end of summer. The young will be able to fly at about forty days of age, and they will move with their parents to these molting lakes, where the adults shed their wing primaries and, for four or five weeks, are flightless. When their wings are restored, they will move in family groups to Izembek Lagoon on the Alaska Peninsula, where they will feed on eelgrass to store up the energy they need to migrate to the coasts of California and Mexico. These movements are repeated every year, with the regularity of seasons. For a brant, the Pacific flyway is something dependably familiar.

But few humans are aware of the existence of the Pacific flyway. It is an entity known to duck hunters, whose sport is regulated by flyway councils composed of game officials concerned about the number of ducks that fly south each fall. A few shorebird biologists investigate where sandpipers rest and feed along the migration routes. But the flyway accom-

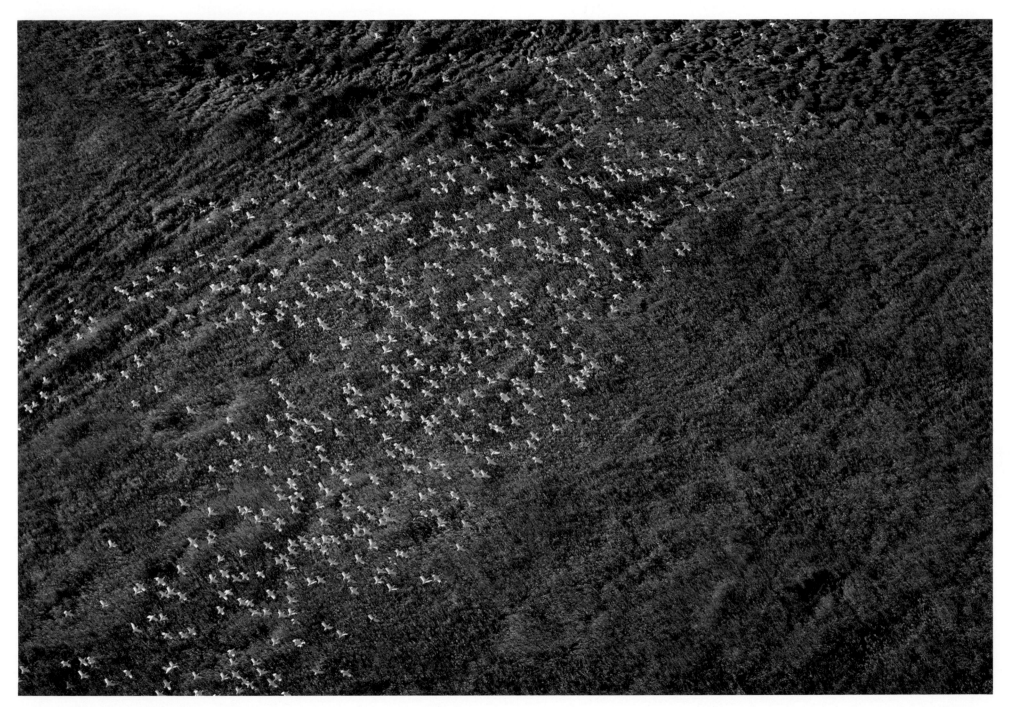

Snow geese, Peace-Athabasca Delta, Alberta, Canada

modates much more than migrating ducks and shore-birds. It hosts sedentary creatures, shy marsh birds, tiny mice, creatures as big as bison and moose. And while most of us express concern for the survival of species, few of us know much about the places we need to preserve to ensure survival. Few of us know where the flyway becomes actual—where those spectacular concentrations of birds drop down through the clouds, touch the earth, and mingle with less-mobile creatures.

The flyway is largely an abstraction, lines drawn on a hemispheric map by waterfowl biologists interested in guessing how many ducks will breed in Canada and Alaska and fly past hunters' guns in ten western states in the fall. It was designed as a way of thinking about ducks, but it works equally well for non-game species like grebes, godwits, phalaropes, and terns. The Pacific flyway is bounded on the west by an indeterminate expanse of Pacific Ocean. Some Alaskan birds fly south to Hawaii and Tahiti. On the east, the flyway is bounded by the Continental Divide from Mexico to Montana, but as the Rockies veer northwest toward the Canadian coast, the flyway boundary streaks northeast to the Athabaska Delta and the Queen Maud Gulf on the Arctic coast. Here, its exact boundaries with the Central flyway grow indistinct, as some birds hatched in the Yukon and northern Alberta may winter in California, while others winter on the Texas Gulf coast on the Central flyway. South of Mexico, the flyway concept exhausts itself in the narrow land bridge of Central America, which concentrates terns and curlews and sandpipers and teals and other long-distance migrants from all four flyways. South of Costa Rica, the long-distance migrants no longer sort out into separate east and west flight lanes.

A map is relatively easy to draw. Finding the flyway on the ground is harder. The birds rarely follow mountain ridges or desert plateaus. They don't frequent our cities or our more intensively farmed rural areas where we have wrung the water out of the landscape. The flyway actually touches the ground only here and there. It is confusing even to birds. You can, in September, watch a flock of curlews come down the San Joaquin Valley, veering east and west and east again, searching for water and looking lost and confused.

If finding the flyway is hard for a curlew, it's harder still for humans. The Pacific flyway is a reflection of the water below the sky. It is a chain of wetlands stretching from the Arctic to the tropics. The term wetland gives us problems. It conjures no visual image. And it encompasses a bewildering variety of landscapes, for wetlands are as varied as the soils, plants, insects, and water that inhabit them. Wetlands may be bogs, marshes, swamps, tide flats, potholes, vernal pools, fens, ponds, bottom lands, cienegas, estuaries, and meadows. Paul Adamus, who devised a system used by the Federal Highway Administration to evaluate wetlands, prefaced his report with a list of 120 such names. Despite this confusion, from north to south there are certain typical landscapes we can look for.

In the far north, beyond the tree line, the flyway comes to earth in tundra. Vast tracts of Alaska, the Yukon, and the Northwest Territories are tundra, a land of wind and ice, low-lying vegetation, and frozen subsoils. The permafrost beneath the surface limits the ground's ability to absorb water, so snow-melt ponds in spring and summer. Much of the land is flat, interrupted only by volcanic cones or dark brown ridges of ice-shattered rock. The wind sweeping off the Bering, Chukchi, and Beaufort seas drives ice crystals and cold, which keep vegetation short. The ground is carpeted with dwarf willow, sedges, lichens, and mosses, things which grow only a few inches into the wind. To walk across this landscape is to walk on the treetops of a miniature forest. Water is abundant. The melted ice and snow dapples the landscape into ponds and muskegs and wanders snakelike in sloughs and rivers. In June, when the sun shines twenty-four hours a day onto much of this water, it brings the ponds and sloughs to life. Algae mats spread across them. Sedges and tussock grasses and pondweeds grow luxuriantly. Mosquitos and black-flies breed in unimaginable numbers. Salmon surge upriver to spawn.

These are Eskimo lands, lands purchased with resolution and endurance by caribou and musk oxen. They are also the great nesting grounds of the north. Vast flocks of snow geese nest on Wrangel and Banks islands. The smaller white Ross' goose nests on the Perry River in Northwest Territories. All the world's eiders, oldsquaws, brant, ruddy turnstones, long-billed dowitchers, red and northern phalropes, sanderlings, red knots and western, Baird's and pectoral sandpipers nest in the Arctic.

To the south and east, where the permafrost vanishes and ice is no longer a barrier to the roots of trees, aspen and spruce line the ponds, and willows grow higher. The northern forest begins here and spreads across the Yukon and Northwest Territories and northern Alberta. It leaps the mountains to the west and stretches down the interior Alaskan valleys of the Yukon and Porcupine rivers. The forest provides cover for moose and deer, which don't venture out onto the tundra. The moose is a wetland creature, seldom venturing far from the streamside willows. The moose support the Cree and Ojibway Indians. The wetlands of the northern forest produce, too, vast numbers of mallard, pintail, scaup, goldeneye, and wigeon that winter in the United States. The rivers host mink, otter, and beaver. The broad delta of the Peace and Athabaska rivers overflows yearly, and nutrients in the floodwaters foster a lush growth of grass that sustains the northernmost race of buffalo. Here, too, is the only breeding population of whooping cranes. It is a land of lush green, sparkling lakes, and tumbling rivers in summer. In the fall, when the leaves vanish and the grass freezes, the land has a ghostly look. The Indians then call it "land of the sticks."

In southern Alberta, the forest gives way to park-like groves of aspen; then the trees vanish, and the land becomes a rolling prairie. It is much like the prairie of the American midwest, snowbound in winter and dry in summer. In spring, the snowmelt gathers in swales gouged out by ancient glaciers. The landscape is dotted with these prairie potholes. All around the potholes, the land is a pale pastel of gray sage and soft yellow grasses. It is the home of antelope and earnest sunlight. A spring day can raise temperatures into the eighties. By summer, many of the ponds dry out, forcing the pintail, wigeon, mallard, and Canada geese that nest on the ponds to march overland to find surviving water. Every few years, drought stalks the pothole country, drying up so many potholes that the ducks, which come off the ponds by the millions in a normal year, fail to breed. The droughts are thought to keep potholes healthy in the long run by controlling plants that would other-

Yukon Flats, Yukon River, Alaska

wise compete with the plants that nurture ducks. But in the short run, there may be sudden population collapses, which are bad news for hunters in the United States. Most of the mallard, pintail, and wigeon that winter in California and Arizona are born on the Alberta prairie.

To the south, the flyway crosses the crest of the Rocky Mountains. In March, you can see pairs of mallards or flocks of snow geese following Montana rivers north toward Alberta. In summer, there are isolated pairs of ducks nesting on the lakes. But the mountains are less important here as a source of wetlands than is the Great Basin to the west. In the Great Basin are saline and alkaline lakes, bodies of water with no outflows, that concentrate salts in the hot summer sun. These lakes produce vast numbers of brine flies, brine shrimp, chironomid midges, and other aquatic creatures, which, in turn, feed huge numbers of migrating birds. The marshes at the outfall of the Bear River on Great Salt Lake are among the most productive waterfowl grounds in the nation. Gray's Lake in Idaho supports a large population of sandhill cranes and, since they have been fostered into the sandhill crane flock, a growing population of whooping cranes. On the western side of the basin, the lakes are surrounded by severe landscapes. Pyramid Lake in Nevada is set in a moonscape of sage and treeless mountain, but it hosts the continent's largest colony of white pelicans. Mono Lake in eastern California and Goose Lake in eastern Oregon look like inland seas, pale and dusty, but they host huge migrating flocks of grebe and phalarope. The Malheur National Wildlife Refuge in Oregon is one of the great waterfowl areas of the nation.

Further to the south, in Nevada, southern Utah, Arizona, and New Mexico, most of the wetlands are riparian. They are river channels and floodplains, old oxbows, and backwaters. Their edges are thronged with cottonwood or tamarisk or mesquite. They host shy rails, bitterns, white-faced ibis, egrets and herons, and large numbers of ducks and geese. The refuges along Utah's Green River serve as broad green oases in the desert. Early Arizona ranchers boasted of good duck hunting on the creeks and rivers. Also important as wetlands in the southwest are spring or seep-fed cienegas, isolated marshlands that are not necessarily connected to creeks or rivers. In northern Arizona, they today provide most of the habitat for aquatic vegetation and insects and so many of the remaining migratory bird habitats.

West of the Sierra and Cascade ranges, from the Fraser River Valley of British Columbia to southern California, warmer coastal valleys and estuaries winter migratory birds in vast numbers. The broad plain of the Skagit River as it drops into Puget Sound hosts large numbers of wintering trumpeter swans. The lower Columbia River and the Willamette Valley of Oregon host most of the dusky and Taverner's Canada geese in winter. In the coast mountains, from the Olympic Range south to the Siskiyous, heavy rains and fogs feed bogs and swamps that are dense with duckweed, wapato, arrowhead, and other marsh plants, and that foster resident populations of wood ducks and mergansers.

As the birds move south from Oregon, they funnel through a gap where the Cascades and Coast Ranges come together. Migrants from the Great Basin and the Canadian potholes also cross the mountain barrier here. Because of this, the Klamath Basin is a kind of avian crossroads, a boulevard stop in the flyway. Every year, it hosts one of the world's most spectacular concentrations of waterfowl. Hundreds of thousands of snow geese arrive from Wrangel Island to loaf on Tule and Klamath Lakes and feed in the surrounding grain fields. They are joined by vast numbers of pintail, mallard, wigeon, white-fronted goose, and Canada goose. The rush of wings as eighty thousand snow geese rise from the lake to feed in a neighboring grain field is a deafening roar, like that of a rocket lifting off a launch pad. The birds fatten here until the first freeze pushes them south. Then they fly over the shoulder of Mount Shasta toward the rocky outcrops of Sutter Buttes, in the heart of California's Central Valley.

The Central Valley was once 500,000 acres of flooded plains in winter. It was lined with channels and sloughs, along which grew deep forests of oak and cottonwood. The valley hosted tule elk— a smaller variety of elk adapted especially to this marshy world—which now survives only on refuges. In the miles and miles of cattail marshes and grassy marshlands were concentrations of duck and geese so thick that early settlers said they blackened the sky. Hunters said they might walk all day and never be out of sight of geese. The valley still receives 40 percent of California's snowmelt and rain runoff, but now the water is shuttled down canals and dredged channels, and most of the wetlands are gone, turned to productive farms and cattle range.

South of the Central Valley, the continuing migrants either leap over to the valley of the Colorado and the Gulf of California, or they move south along the coast of Mexico. Most of Mexico's western interior is too dry to provide much wetland habitat, but along the coast there are rich wintering grounds for waterfowl and shorebirds.

The Pacific coast is a flyway unto itself. From the western Arctic to Costa Rica, the coast links together a continuous strand of wetlands. Along the Arctic, these wetlands are mostly tundra, sedge marsh, and tide flat. Southeast of Anchorage, the Copper River Delta's tide flats of glacial silt gather as many as eleven million shorebirds each May. There are western sandpipers and dunlins from Mexico, surfbirds and golden plovers from Hawaii, and bristle-thighed curlews that have flown all the way from Tahiti. In a year, the Copper River Delta may host twenty million migrants. It is also the sole breeding ground of the dusky Canada goose.

South of Alaska's Copper River there are few coastal wetlands, because the mountains rise out of the sea and the coastal valleys are still occupied by living glaciers. Few large rivers flow into the sea or build up deltas that harbor wetlands. There are small enclave wetlands, like the 4,000-acre Mendenhall Wetlands at Juneau, where several hundred Canada geese nest, where Dolly Varden char and salmon spend much of their lives, and where bald eagles congregate to fish. It is not until the migrants reach British Columbia's Fraser River Valley, however, that a broad coastal estuary opens up. The Fraser once hosted vast numbers of ducks and geese and cranes. Today, most of its wetlands have been diked and drained for agricultural purposes.

To the south, Puget Sound with its vast expanses of river valleys and tidelands is an important staging area for migrating shorebirds and waterfowl. Along the coast farther south are Grays Harbor, Willapa Bay, Humboldt Bay, Tomales Bay, Bolinas Lagoon, and San Francisco Bay, all important wintering grounds for migratory birds. San Francisco Bay is the largest

Green-winged teal, Old Crow Flats, Yukon Territory, Canada

wintering and staging area for shorebirds along the coast. More than 70 percent of the shorebirds using the flyway stage or winter or breed there. "It's the major refueling and resting place for birds on the Pacific flyway," says Roger Johnson, manager of the San Francisco Bay National Wildlife Refuge. "There's no other place of any greater significance on the Pacific coast." It seems more valuable than Puget Sound because it is shallow and therefore more conductive of solar energy than the sound. South of San Francisco, the central California coast grows again steep and rocky and broken by few large rivers, so there are few wetlands. South of Point Conception, however, the continental shelf does not drop off so steeply, and broad sandy beaches form. Here, there were once dozens of extensive coastal marshes. At the turn of the century, the marshes of the Los Angeles area hosted more than a hundred duck hunting clubs. But most of the marshes have since been diked and filled. There are remnants at Morro Bay, Newport Bay, San Diego Bay, Mission Bay, and Tiajuana Slough, all of which host wintering birds. And all along the coast from the Aleutians to Mexico are nearshore waters that host winter loons, grebes, and scoters that have bred on the freshwater wetlands of the Canadian interior and the Great Basin.

As the migrants follow the coast south into Mexico, the wetlands change markedly. In place of the salt marsh pickleweed of California's coast, there are mangrove swamps. Mangroves are immensely fertile areas, but because they lack the grassier plants of the north, they don't appeal as grandly to the northern ducks and geese. Ninety percent of the continent's black brant winter in the coastal lagoons of the Baja California Peninsula, especially in Laguna Scammon and Baja Magdalena, where the eelgrass they feed on in the north still grows. The bald eagle may even nest in mangrove. Blue- and green-winged teal winter all the way into South America. But most of the pintails and mallards winter north of the Mexican border. In places, the more typical duck is a tree duck, a bird with legs farther back on its body and capable of perching on mangrove branches. Nevertheless, the coastal lagoons and tide flats of the mainland offer dozens of rich wintering grounds that attract northern ducks and shorebirds. Tens of thousands of redheads and lesser scaups and the

southernmost buffleheads and red-headed mergansers winter at Laguna Agiambampo on the southern coast of Sonora. At Ensenada del Pabellon, scaups dive for molluscs amid schools of porpoise and against a backdrop of mangrove. The mud flats at Ensenada del Pabellon host large numbers of shorebirds, and in the mangroves are pelicans and frigatebirds. At the Marismas Nacionales, a complex of lagoons between Mazatlan and San Blas, there are sandy beaches between stands of mangrove and acacia. The molluscs produced in these areas entice hundreds of thousands of northern shovellers. Large numbers of green-winged teal and lesser scaup also winter here.

If the bolder outlines of the flyway, just described, seem clear, things begin to blur when we look closer. Within even a single region of the flyway, there may be enormous differences in wetlands. Two cienegas a few miles apart in Arizona or two potholes in southern Alberta may look very much alike, but only one may host waterfowl. Some of the lakes on the west slope of the Rocky Mountains host trumpeter swans, while other lakes, apparently identical, do not. The chemistry of the soil or of the water may be different, and that may foster different plant and insect life. Water levels may be a few inches too high or a few inches too low to support a critical food item at a particular time of the year. It is thought that ducks nesting on prairie potholes require two or three different potholes to rear a brood. Newly hatched ducklings need insects and other invertebrates as a source of protein. The shallow ponds that best provide invertebrates may dry out early in summer, forcing the ducks to march overland a mile or two to the next surviving pothole. Later in life, ducklings need the carbohydrates in plant food to amass the energy they will need for migration, and that may require a different kind of pond.

While ducks and clapper rails can recognize the wetlands they need for survival, we humans may not. We don't really know where the flyway touches the ground. Some valuable wetlands may not even look to us like wetlands. That is something Paul Kelly, a biologist with the California Department of Fish and Game, worries much about.

Around the edges of San Francisco Bay are areas that seem unconnected to the bay and devoid of water most of the year. They are lands that were used

as pasture or duck hunting clubs when California cities still had a lot of land to expand into. But today, as the cities around the bay grow crowded, developers want to build on these lands. They are easily diked and drained. And the stakes of development are often high. A single acre of San Jose marshland sold in 1985 for one million dollars. Such high stakes, Kelly has discovered, pose a threat to the flyway.

For in February and March, these seasonal wetlands fill with rainwater and suddenly bloom. Billions of aquatic plants and invertebrates come to life in them, and these feed millions of ducks, shorebirds, herons, cormorants, pelicans, kingfishers, terns, gulls, stilts, and avocets. Says Kelly, "Ecologists always portrayed the salt marsh as the ultimate ecosystem. Certainly for herring and crab and fish it is the ultimate. But for the birds their needs are more diverse." On these seasonal wetlands, says Kelly, "I could show you ten thousand eared grebes and thousands of dabbling ducks. You'd never see anything like that in a salt marsh. Some bird species don't even use the bay. They just use the seasonal wetlands. Phalarope, white pelican, avocets, stilts, eared grebes, Bonaparte's gulls—they use the salt ponds, not the bay. By far the majority of dabbling ducks are on the salt ponds. Most of the diving ducks are on the ponds. We have more water birds on non-tidal areas than on tidal areas, more in numbers and in kinds."

Seventy-five percent of the bay's wetlands have already been filled, lost under military bases, airport runways, housing tracts, and garbage dumps. In 1966, Bay Area voters established the Bay Conservation and Development Commission (BCDC) to stop unrestricted filling of the bay. It was thought that wildlife would survive if bay surface was protected. The BCDC today has jurisdiction over filling seaward from existing dikes. And the U.S. Army Corps of Engineers has jurisdiction over filling of lands behind the dikes. The seasonal wetlands Kelly worries about are behind the dikes. And the corps, which has little concern for wildlife, doesn't always agree with Kelly, the Department of Fish and Game, or the Fish and Wildlife Service as to what constitutes a wetland.

Both the Fish and Wildlife Service and the Corps of Engineers recognize as a wetland any place that has waterlogged soils or plants characteristic of waterlogged soils. Both agencies have official lists of aquatic

White pelicans, Slave River, N.W.T., Canada

plants they regard as indicator species. But developers have gotten around the corps' definition by draining and discing the land, actions which the corps doesn't regard as filling, but which effectively remove the aquatic plants. Once the water and the plants are gone, the developer maintains that the site is not a wetland under the corps' definitions and goes ahead and fills.

Because increasing development pressure has collided with declining wetland habitat, deciding what is a wetland and what is not has become a complex and embittering problem. Since the 1960s, we have charged various state and federal agencies with protection of one aspect or another of wetlands. The Corps of Engineers has responsibility for regulating wetlands adjacent to, or connected to, navigable waterways. The Fish and Wildlife Service has responsibility for wetlands considered valuable to wildlife, but it cannot contest a corps permit. The Environmental Protection Agency (EPA) can dispute a corps decision over what constitutes a wetland. State fish and game agencies have interests in particular kinds of wetlands, and some administer their own waterfowl breeding areas. Coastal states have coastal zone management programs that contain wetland protection provisions. The U.S. Department of Transportation has a policy of trying to protect wetlands when it builds federal highways. The U.S. Forest Service and the Bureau of Land Management have a variety of wetland policies. All these agencies, however, have their own ways of defining wetlands. Some define them by proximity to tidal waters. Some flood-control districts define wetlands as areas subject to annual floods, while others define them as areas subject to 100-year floods. In Connecticut, wetlands are defined as including sites with poorly drained soils. In Washington, the shoreline program defines wetlands as including a 200-foot strip beyond the high-water mark of specified bodies of water. Oregon definitions in 1986 encompassed submerged vegetation but excluded emergent vegetation, a distinction that left out the wooded ponds around Portland that produce wood ducks and mergansers. With such conflicting definitions and multiple jurisdictions, our problems defining wetlands are magnified.

To try to reduce the confusion, the U.S. Fish and Wildlife Service has been trying to map and type wet-

lands throughout the United States. Its most recent effort, the National Wetlands Inventory, began in 1974. By 1979, the service had developed a classification scheme that typed wetlands in complex categories, such as "estuarine, intertidal, emergent wetland—persistent", or "palustrine, scrub-shrub wetland" or "lacustrine, littoral, unconsolidated shore, subclass mud, seasonally flooded, with hypersaline water and mineral soil." The terms make little anecdotal sense to anybody but an ecologist or a soil specialist, but the system is an excellent way of describing, mapping, and quantifying wetlands.

However, the terms are simply bothersome to developers who are less interested in water regimes and soil chemistries than in the commercial potential that can be raised over such things. The National Wetlands Inventory intended to use geological survey maps, aerial photos, historical data, and on-the-spot inspections to plot the nation's wetlands onto inventory maps. Such maps would help inform developers and local planners of the ecological and hydrological values of the land. They would also help conservationists argue against Corps of Engineers permits. But by 1986, finally, maps had been published only for New Jersey and Delaware. Mapping had stopped in most of the western states until the states could come up with funds to help pay for the mapping. And even where the Fish and Wildlife Service hoped to push through maps for particularly controversial areas, such as San Francisco Bay, developers tried to stall publication of the maps.

State officials have sought to inventory their own wetlands. David Brown of the Arizona Department of Game and Fish completed his own study of Arizona's wetlands in 1985. The California Assembly Resources Subcommittee completed a study of the status and trends of California wetlands in 1984, but did not produce maps. The Alberta Provincial Game Department prepares maps indicating the quality of waterfowl habitat, a fair approximation of the kinds of data assembled by the National Wetlands Inventory in the United States. But elsewhere, inventories have stalled. David Lockman of the Wyoming Department of Game and Fish proposed an inventory and managed to complete a survey of one river drainage, but could get no more funding. Ducks Unlimited is using Landsat photographs to prepare its own

wetlands inventory, but that effort aims at preserving duck habitat and may ignore wetlands valuable for fish, non-game birds, flood control, and water quality.

In the end, we are still a long way from agreeing on what constitutes a wetland. In Los Angeles, an EPA official says, only half-jokingly, "Abandoned shopping carts are a good indicator species of wetlands," because people dump them in river channels, some of which are not yet encased in concrete. In San Francisco, a state official suggests, "If the developer across the table has a lawyer sitting next to him, then it's a wetland. Otherwise he wouldn't have his lawyer with him."

Finding the Pacific flyway is mostly a matter of finding wetlands. We do that by looking for birds or water or aquatic vegetation. But we haven't yet acquired a common understanding of what plants or water or birds identify a wetland. So, locating the flyway and speaking for it remains largely a matter of abstractions. Few of us recognize the flyway when we see it.

While we try to sort out our confusions, the wetlands of the Pacific flyway have become extremely controversial. Almost anywhere there is a wetland in the west today, there is a conflict between commerce and wildlife. Our language is not equal to the demands of the conflict. Our understanding of wetlands is blunted by our househabit, our lack of experience with the out-of-doors, and a lack of biological study. But our greatest handicap is a cultural prejudice about what happens when water and earth come together.

Canvasback, Yukon Flats, Alaska

Gray wolf, Peace-Athabasca Delta, Alberta, Canada

Gray wolf track, Slave River, N.W.T., Canada

Old Crow Flats, Yukon Territory, Canada

Moose, Liard River, British Columbia, Canada

Richardson Mountains, Yukon Territory, Canada

Tundra swans, Peace-Athabasca Delta, Alberta, Canada

Peace-Athabasca Delta, Alberta, Canada

White-winged scoter, Peace-Athabasca Delta, Alberta, Canada

Yukon Flats, Alaska

Wood bison, Peace-Athabasca Delta, Alberta, Canada

Peace-Athabasca Delta, Alberta, Canada

Lesser yellowlegs, Ogilvie Mountains, Yukon Territory, Canada

For most people, the problem with wetlands is that when water comes to rest on earth, it makes mud. Most people don't like mud. Not Fred Nichols. Nichols likes to be up to his ankles in mud, digging around for clams and oysters. In hip waders and aviator glasses and a brushy mustache, Nichols is an odd sight on the edges of San Francisco Bay. Each step he takes is plodding. He rocks a foot a little to free it from the mud, and places it flat in front of him, sinking almost to his knees as he shifts his weight. His progress is like that of a crane.

Nichols is a biologist working for the U.S. Geological Survey, and the area of his keenest interest is the health of San Francisco Bay. He knows bay muds the way some people know movie stars or classical music. "San Pablo Bay mud west of Tubbs Island is very soft stuff," he says. "It has no grit to it. It's fine mud that's mostly coming out of the Sacramento River. It's molded by wind and waves into ridges. Over by Hayward, it gets that west wind, and it's sandy—sand with mud in it, so it's different." And he knows that mud changes constantly. "New channels open up. It grows in some places and shrinks in other places. It's highly dynamic." He says old Indian accounts suggested that a river of fresh water flowed all the way through the Golden Gate as little as four thousand years ago. "The geological evidence is that the estuary is only ten thousand years old," he says. Hydraulic mining in the nineteenth century raised the bottom of San Pablo Bay a meter, and the marsh grew a mile in a year.

Nichols is interested in mud because he believes it is the foundation of biological life in the bay. "Our contention is that, as opposed to the long-held belief that marshes provide most of the organic matter in an estuarine ecosystem, most of the organic matter here is provided by the mud flat." Mud flats mix water, oxygen, and mineral matter, and because even at high tide the water is shallow (half the bay is less than six feet deep), there is lots of solar energy. The bay produces huge amounts of organic matter, and, says Nichols, much of that "is coming on the tides off the mud flat and settling on the salt marsh."

Nichols is interested in what lives in the mud and how that, too, changes. "The single most important fishery in the 1890s was oysters," he says. "It crashed. By the 1930s it was dead. Anecdotal accounts suggest it succumbed to pollution. The oysters tasted foul. They didn't grow very well." But there might have been other causes. A storm in 1862 virtually flushed all the salt water out of San Francisco Bay. "The tide didn't reverse in the Golden Gate for two weeks. Thirty inches of rain fell in the month of January alone—more than a year's normal total for San Francisco. Did that wipe out the native shellfish? Did that set the stage for the introduction of exotic species? We just don't know."

The native San Francisco Bay oyster was small and had a coppery taste that the Forty-Niners didn't much like. Oysters were shipped to San Francisco from Puget Sound, Mexico, and Japan, but importation was a marginal business because most of the shellfish died on the way. In 1869, with the opening of the transcontinental railway, entrepreneurs began to ship boxcars full of live oysters from the east coast. The live oysters had "spat," or larval oysters, clinging to their shells. The entrepreneurs simply threw the live oysters into the bay, and the larvae grew. The east coast oyster never reproduced in the bay, so the oystermen had to keep replenishing the stock. A number of exotic organisms also clung to the shells and they *did* reproduce in the bay. Other marine species came on the keels or in the bilgewater of sailing ships. Today, says Nichols, "Perhaps 99 percent of the species here are introduced." He recites a list of names of mudsnails and clams, and then wonders what happened to the natives that were here before them. He also marvels at how hospitable the bay has been to immigrants. "Thirty to thirty-five species of clam alone live right here," he says. There is so much food in bay mud that Nichols has found up to 400,000

Canvasback male, Buffalo Lake, Alberta, Canada

Gemma gemma clams, a small introduced species, per square meter of mud. Of the forty species of fish that frequent Suisun Bay, twenty are introduced. "We're always getting new species of shrimp in the north bay from China," he says. "In the late 1960s, the most recent introduction of a mollusc came in the algae they brought with lobsters into restaurants on Fisherman's Wharf."

Despite all these exotic species, the bay is remarkably healthy. It feeds millions of migrating birds, serves as a nursery for bass, sturgeon, and salmon, and provides enough microorganisms to control phytoplankton blooms triggered by sewage pollution. "We're convinced," says Nichols, "that the animals that live on the bottom can consume enough of the plants so that they don't accumulate. All the conditions are right for us to have more algae in the water column than we can account for. Circumstantial evidence says the animals are eating them. We are convinced that these animals out in the flats are highly critical in preventing eutrophication. Acute pollution that killed the animals might give us eutrophication and nuisance blooms."

Few people share Nichol's fascination with mud. In twelve years of working in bay mud, he says, "We see joggers and fishermen waiting for high tide. But few people come out here." The reason is that mud, to the human mind, is nature's least congenial setting. We cavort in ocean waves, bask in desert sun, and brave the ice of mountain peaks. But mud we leave to clammers and trench soldiers. We think of mud as something unfinished, a lugubrious prospect that goes with heavy skies and deferred purposes, plasma waiting to become land or water. Either it will flood or it will dry out. Marshes and estuaries silt in and become meadows. Winter floods turn them into lakes or bays.

More often, we'll do the job ourselves: we'll dredge up the mud or dike it and dry it out. Those who come out to the bay, says Nichols, come chiefly to change the mud. Mud is prime real estate to developers of industrial parks, housing tracts, and marinas. In the 1850s, rotting ships were sunk on San Francisco's waterfront to provide fill for new real estate. Developers building high rises today often unearth the bones of these ships five blocks from the present waterfront. Similar filling spread all around the bay, until more than a third of it was filled. Today, most of the military bases, airports, and garbage dumps—and many of the housing tracts and industrial parks—are on filled land. Traditionally, people have looked upon bay mud as something wasted by nature. On San Francisco Bay, the Corps of Engineers is the chief regulatory agency. Says Nichols, "The engineers have said, 'There's all that mud out there. What do we need all that mud for?'"

In fact, mud is extremely purposeful. It is a lively place, one of those rare edges where sun, earth, and water come together, and the combination authors whole libraries of life. Mud is made of fine clay particles, organic debris, and water. The clay particles are electrically charged, and organic chemicals adhere to them. Microbes adhere, too, so there may be billions of bacteria, fungi, and other single-celled creatures in a cubic inch of bay mud. There are batteries of cells siphoning organic chemicals out of the soup and spitting their own novel chemicals back in. Scientists now think it was in mud, rather than in seawater, that life on earth began.

Life concentrates near the surface, where there is air, light, and fresh debris. On the surface, mud may be sulfury yellow because of all this chemical commerce. Slice open a cross section of a clam's burrow and you'll see it is lined with brown mud, even though the waterlogged and organically poor mud around it is the color of charcoal. Below the surface, because there is less oxygen, there is less active commerce, and the mud may be as black as asphalt. But even there, anaerobic bacteria fabricate methane and other chemicals. The anaerobes are important, for they may break down 30 percent of the organic matter in a marsh, recycling molecules that once made up cord grass and cattail for use by other creatures. They also serve as food for larger microbes and insect larvae.

The microbial life is not plain to see, but it is evident to the trained eye. At low tide, the mud of San Francisco Bay glows bright gold from a slick of diatoms, starburst-shaped single-celled creatures that thrive in the shallow water. Isolated salt ponds in the nearby marshes have patches of rust-red mud where bacteria liberate sulfur from seawater. On the water surface are oil-like sheens of bacteria clinging to minute particles of metal that they have liberated from the mud and water.

We are more likely to notice the larger creatures. There are worms, insect larvae, crustaceans, molluscs. Bent-nosed clams snuggle six inches down into the mud, scything with the sharp edge of their shells to burrow deeper. They extend siphons to the surface to browse for food, leaving starlike tracks on the mud that attract feeding godwits and willets. Horse mussels cluster around the roots of cord grass and, in spring, broadcast a soup of eggs onto the tide. At times, there is so much life on the flats that they are pebbled as far as the eye can see with grazing dog whelks. When the tide comes in, bat rays and flounder, crabs and young bass feed over the rich mud. When the tide goes out, shorebirds by the thousand flock to dine on worms and clams.

It isn't just tidal flats that do this. Behind the dikes along the edges of the bay are salt ponds and pasture lands that remain dry nine or ten months out of the year. But when the rains come, these low-lying areas pond deeply with runoff, and they, too, come alive. Billions of tiny crustaceans hatch from cysts in the mud. Worms and clams and insect larvae come to life. And millions of diving ducks, wading birds, and gulls descend on these seasonal wetlands to feed.

It has always been thought that the marshes that fringe our coastal tide flats are the most productive parts of our wetlands. But research on San Francisco Bay suggests that it is the life that washes up from the mud flats that feeds the marshes. The mussels above the tideline, the barnacles on their backs, the isopods burrowing among the roots of cord grass, the hundreds of faceless worms and insect larvae, all wait for the tide to float them whatever broths have been cooking on the mud flats. "They're teeming with life," says Ron Oremland of the Geological Survey. "They're like the coral reefs of the estuary." The detritus that then washes off both mud flat and marsh feeds dozens of species of fish. Up to 70 percent of the primary productivity of a coastal wetland may be exported in the form of detritus and juvenile fish and shellfish to open water areas. Studies in Alaska show 50 percent more invertebrate biomass in estuarine streams than in forest streams just above them. And

Franklin's gulls, Buffalo Lake, Alberta, Canada

salmon depend upon that estuarine mud to produce food during the critical period when they reside in estuaries, waiting for their bodies to adapt to salt water. We have worried much about what the dams on the Columbia and the Sacramento have done to salmon stocks; we have not paid sufficient attention to what the diking of salt marshes and tide flats—and the acid leachate from log booms at river mouths—have done to the estuarine food supplies of juvenile fish.

So rich and lively are muds that each can be said to have its own personality. There are soft, jellylike muds of the deep bays that no one can walk on. There are sandy muds that can support the weight of a truck. The mud of San Francisco Bay is, in places, almost like soup. On Alaska's Mendenhall Wetlands, the mud is so sandy that walking on it is like walking on a beach. There are peats—beds of plant litter, which, trapped in the airlessness of a bog, do not decompose. There are seasonal pools of rainwater, lush with algae in winter, cracked and dry in summer. There are butter-yellow muds, oily black muds, muds the color of coffee or the blue of sky, gray volcanic muds slumping down mountain valleys, not yet impregnated with life. Each derives from different rocks and is liquefied by water passing through different soils, bringing to it different salts and minerals. Each mud has its own chemistry, and each nurtures its own microscopic flora and fauna.

Non-western people often know how varied muds are. In Africa and Indonesia, people eat bits of mud and clay as a delicacy. They are choosy about which muds they eat, for each has its own taste and its own risk of intestinal parasites or mineral toxins. In 1788, La Perouse found that Javanese villagers sold flat loaves of reddish earth that the natives, especially pregnant women, ate. I. H. N. Evans found women in Borneo eating a hard, dark purple clay that they dug out of the bluish gray clay of a riverbank. A nineteenth-century traveler observed, "The Persians have trained their taste to such an extent that they discriminate between various kinds of clay without hesitation." Alexander von Humboldt wrote that "in Guinea, the Negroes eat a yellowish earth which they call *caouac*. When carried as slaves to the West Indies, they try to procure there a similar earth."

Studies of English peats suggest what geophagists find in mud. Sphagnum peat may be 6 percent sugar—richer than laboratory media used to grow microorganisms. So rich are peats in organic chemicals that, when removed from bogs, they foster huge populations of microbes; that is why gardeners favor them as fertilizer. And so rich are the microbe colonies that peat generates its own heat. You can raise the temperature by adding hay, because that increases the activity of the microbes.

Mud is essential to a considerable portion of the life we are familiar with. It is what makes the flyways work. At least 75 percent of our bird species depend at some time on wetlands for breeding, staging, feeding, or loafing. Without mud, that great river of birds that passes back and forth across our skies in fall and spring would dry up. Mud is the heart of our fisheries. Of nearly three million marine fish caught by U.S. recreational and commercial fishermen in 1980, two-thirds were wetland-dependent species. Salmon require estuaries for part of their life cycle. Largemouth bass spawn in temporarily flooded zones of bottomland hardwood, so that the fry can feed on the huge invertebrate populations. Walleye, bluegill, bass, crappie, pickerel, and muskelunge are commonly found in vegetated wetlands, which offer food and protection from predators, sunlight, and strong currents. Juvenile marine fish and shellfish use coastal marshes because the salinity level excludes saltwater and freshwater predators. Eight of the fifteen most important commercial fish and shellfish in the U.S.—including shrimp, salmon, menhaden, flounder, oyster, clam, blue crab, and dungeness crab—are wetland-dependent.

Even some large carnivores are wetland-dependent. Wolves in the north woods subsist in part upon moose, which are wetland creatures. In California's Central Valley, grizzlies once fed on tule elk, a marshland species. Along the northern Pacific coast, brown bears depend upon salmon running up the rivers for food during part of the year. The bears feeding on salmon in Alaska's McNeil River appear so dependably that wildlife photographers cluster there also, and to reduce camera pressure on the spot, the Alaska Department of Fish and Game has instituted a lottery for limited passes to the river.

And there are values that arise out of simply having places where mud can accumulate. In places, wetlands are necessary for flood control. Wetlands are wetlands because that is where the water goes. We dike them or channelize them to move the water away and then build houses over their remains. Then along comes a 100-year flood and we find that the engineering was inadequate, or that we simply moved a flood problem downstream. Studies of a 90-acre cypress-tupelo swamp on the Cache River watershed in Illinois showed that it retained 8.4 percent of the watershed's runoff during floods. The Corps of Engineers estimated that the loss of all 8,422 acres of wetlands in Massachusetts' Charles River Basin would result in flood damages of over seventeen million dollars a year. Studies at the Agassiz National Wildlife Refuge in Minnesota showed that floodwater went into the refuge's wetlands at a rate of 5,000 cubic feet per second, but came out at 1,400 cubic feet per second, and that the wetland thus reduced the flood peak at Crookston, downstream, by 1.5 feet.

Another benefit of muddy places is groundwater recharge. Water spread out over a broad area will percolate into the underground water table more rapidly than water moving down a narrow channel. Since half the nation's drinking water comes from wells, recharge may be a critically under-appreciated function of wetlands. In California's Central Valley, pumping of groundwater to irrigate farms removes two million acre-feet more water from the ground each year than natural runoff replenishes. The floodplains that covered the valley are gone, so much less water seeps back into the ground than did a century ago. In places, the underground waterbearing rock has crumpled, and the land surface has subsided more than twenty feet. That means much of the aquifer can no longer hold water, and that farmers must drill deeper wells and pay higher energy costs for water. It also means that eventually there could be no more groundwater to farm with.

Muddy places are also helpful in maintaining the quality of water. By slowing water movement, precipitating out solids and subjecting them to the action of microbes in the mud, wetlands can remove toxic and disease-carrying substances. Plants in wetlands may take up dissolved phosphorus and nitrogen

Gadwall, Buffalo Lake, Alberta, Canada

and so reduce biological oxygen demand, leaving the water fresher downstream. Studies in Texas suggest that DDT is broken down only in wetland environments. With increasing use of pesticides and toxic industrial solvents, the value of wetlands to water quality may increase. Don May of Friends of the Earth in Los Angeles has done an inventory of local wetlands. Many of them are terribly polluted. One creek, he says, caught fire and burned down an iron overpass. But, May says, Byxbie Marsh, a section of creek left unchannelized when local flood-control agencies couldn't get the landowner to allow them to corset it in concrete, cleanses such water. "The water," says May, "when it comes into this area, is a milky color. It smells of analine. The flood-control channels of concrete above it are often etched with sulfuric acids and other industrial waste." By the time the water passes through the marsh, it has lost the smell and regained clarity. Says May, "One of the main functions the marsh performs is to keep the pollution from going down channel. Of the thirteen categories of substances the water quality people are concerned about, all of them are screened out by wetlands. What comes out is very close to potable water quality."

Mud may also have effects on weather. Drained agricultural lands in Florida were five degrees Fahrenheit colder in winter and more subject to frost than undrained lands. They were also five degrees warmer in summer. There is some concern in Florida that, because thunderclouds rise off the larger lakes, drainage of wetlands may reduce thundershower activity, and thus reduce the amount of water percolating into the shallow aquifers that Florida relies upon for drinking supplies.

But the world is blind to the life and beauty and utility of mud. We have few kind words for mud. It is what we sling when we want to besmirch a politician or a movie star. Confused ideas are said to be muddy. So is bad coffee. Most of our words for mud sound like expletives: bog, swamp, fen, mire, muck. The words suggest the strain of mud on human composure. We are purposeful and airy beings, and we want our movements to be quick and uninhibited, full of breeze and whim. But a determined mud won't let you hurry. You move as if under a heavy burden.

You put one foot down and it slips away. You lift the other, but it is stuck. You rock back and forth, arguing with suction, trying to explain movement to mud. In the end, you neither edify nor finesse it. You slog through by main strength and curses.

We don't think mud is much to look at either. Brown is the color of things thrown together, of decay, of spent hopes and used-up light. Mud has no edge or impulse. It doesn't stand up or sing. We are apt to look at it, if at all, through clouds of mosquitoes or shrouds of mist.

In the modern world, mud has few defenders, chiefly because we no longer think of it as a part of nature but regard it as a cultural symbol of abasement, disorder, and confusion. Mud becomes symbolic easily, because it obscures the outlines and intentions of things. Leviticus declares: "All that have not fins and scales in the sea and in the rivers, they shall be an abomination unto you." The implication is that things that dwell in the mud and therefore have no need to be seen and so have no shiny scales or sharp outlines are morally ambiguous. We humans live mainly by our eyes and declare our intentions with body postures and warning lights. Sharp outlines are important. We don't really fear clams and isopods. We fear the intentions of other humans. And as society becomes more differentiated by race and caste, class and clique, we grow to fear an increasing number of ambiguities. Sexuality, race, and moral confusions obscure our edges. And mud becomes a metaphor for this confusion. Elizabethan writers spoke of "muddy brained peasants" and "the muddy and tumultuous suggestions of the flesh." Tennyson described illicit pleasures as "mudhoney." Eighteenth-century slaveholders clapped metal mouthlocks on slaves caught eating mud and regarded geophagy as subversion. Today, female mud wrestling delights spectators in our seamier night clubs by blurring the margins of sexuality, individuality, and violence all at once.

In our confusion between muddy minds and muddy grounds, we have made war on biological mud. Most of our coastal settlements arose in wetlands, and as they expanded, we filled in marsh and tide flat. One tenth of the United States was once wetland. But to make those lands convenient to farm, to

keep water from choking crops and swales from confining machinery, to obliterate the moral ambiguities from the air round us, we filled and leveled and drained the land. Half our original wetlands are gone. More than 90 percent of California's wetlands are gone. So are more than 90 percent of Connecticut's and 95 percent of Iowa's. Eighty percent of the wetlands of the Mississippi Delta are gone. The U.S. Fish and Wildlife Service predicts that at the current rate of loss, there will simply be no waterfowl habitat left in one hundred years.

Even where muds aren't being filled or drained, they are being abused. Our bays and estuaries are increasingly repositories for chemical wastes. Bay muds now carry heavy burdens of cadmium, lead, chromium, arsenic, mercury, and pesticides. The clams and mussels of San Francisco Bay accumulate these toxins readily, and in some areas are declared unfit to eat. Research has yet to show conclusively whether birds and fish are affected by this pollution. But striped bass populations in San Francisco Bay are only 10 percent of what they were twenty years ago, and much of the evidence points to chemical pollution as the cause. Lead shot left in the marshes of our wildlife refuges by hunters is thought to kill at least 2 percent of the ducks and geese using the Pacific flyway. Such alarming levels of selenium are now found in the tissues of ducks in San Francisco Bay that hunters are warned by the State Department of Health Services not to eat the scoters they shoot.

It is a trend that could bring us deeper tragedy. If we pave over our tidelands or pickle their microbes in industrial chemicals, we might eliminate the creatures that consume algae in our bays and rivers. Nuisance phytoplankton blooms would accelerate. And in the oxygen-depleted waters, fish and wildlife would decline. We would be left with the heavy stench of sewage and rotting plants.

Or worse. Orie Loucks of Butler University observes that mud is one of the earth's largest repositories of carbon. Plants and animals that die and sink into mud are incompletely decomposed. Says Loucks, "There are huge organic accumulations along tropical coasts and at the mouths of tropical rivers." As we drain wetlands, the carbon is exposed to new forms of bacteria, which oxidize it and release it into

Canvasback female, Buffalo Lake, Alberta, Canada

the atmosphere. Increased atmospheric carbon seals in solar heat. Already, the carbon released by our destruction of forests and burning of fossil fuels is known to have raised global temperatures. As this warming continues, there will be melting of polar ice caps and changes in rainfall and cropping patterns. Loucks believes 10 to 15 percent of the increase we have already seen in atmospheric carbon may be due to the draining of wetlands. Changing the mud may change our climate.

Mud is not place or object. It is part of the process of life. It is what happens to the ground after it rains. It is what keeps rivers and lakes and estuaries lively. It breathes oxygen, birds, and insects into the sky. Obscure, uncelebrated, unloved, mud is nevertheless part of the music of life. There is beauty and elegance in it, in the sheen of light on top of it, in the persistence of water clinging to it, in the arterial pattern of channel and rill. Some of us find in tide flats and marshes a feeling of time and space and solitude, a sense that life moves with liquid ease and gravity, browsing a channel here, filling a channel there, absolving us of haste and rocky purpose. If we can overcome our cultural prejudices against it, mud can catch the eye and stir the heart. It is a measure of our patience with the world. If we can bring ourselves to leave it alone, to let it ooze and dessicate and slump and mumble at its own pace, there is hope for us as a species.

Marshes, Buffalo Lake, Alberta, Canada

Marbled godwit, Brooks, Alberta, Canada

Redhead, ruddy, and scaup, Brooks, Alberta, Canada

Longtail weasel, Brooks, Alberta, Canada

Northern shoveler duckling, Brooks, Alberta, Canada

Mallard, Buffalo Lake, Alberta, Canada

Blue-winged teal, Buffalo Lake, Alberta, Canada

Northern pintail, Brooks, Alberta, Canada

American avocet, Brooks, Alberta, Canada

Aspen Parklands, Buffalo Lake, Alberta, Canada

Beaver, Buffalo Lake, Alberta, Canada

Willet, Brooks, Alberta, Canada

Yellow-headed blackbird, Brooks, Alberta, Canada

Horned grebe, Brooks, Alberta, Canada

Snow geese, Brooks, Alberta, Canada

In 1779, Captain Cook brought his ship, *Resolution,* to anchor in Kealakekua Bay on the island of Hawaii to repair a broken mast. There was a skirmish with the natives, and Captain Cook was killed. The Hawaiians dismembered his corpse and subsequently returned only parts of it, which the British sailors silently lowered to its final resting place in the bay. Today, a pale-white cement obelisk rises from the scrub-covered cliffs on the bay's inaccessible north shore, commemorating Cook's untimely departure. Below the cliffs are caves containing the bones of ancient Hawaiians—perhaps, too, the unreturned bones of the sea captain. A young American transient who had slept in the caves told me about the bones one spring morning as we sat in the dazzling sunshine along the bay's southern shore.

Kealakekua Bay seemed much as it must have appeared two hundred years before. Coco palms lined the shore. A thick growth of koa and lantana walled off the gentle surf, and the ground beneath the scrub was a jumble of hardened lava, torturous to walk upon. There had been little construction by the bay, little of the tourist development that has so urbanized most of Hawaii. So there had been little of the silting and sedimentation that choked many of Hawaii's finest coral reefs. The reef here was still timelessly beautiful, the water clear and full of bright butterfly fish, colorful wrasses, dark sea urchins, elegant pastel parrot fishes, moray eels, sea turtles, and huge manta rays gliding coolly through the water. Dolphins came into the bay and leapt by the hundreds under a rainbow.

It was low tide, time for gathering food from a healthy reef. A Hawaiian couple—he in bright-blue cotton-print shirt and she in an electrifying red muumuu, the hem of which she held daintily out of the water—walked in the shallows. They were immensely dignified people, with broad shoulders and strong jaws, clear eyes and glistening skin. They waded slowly in the shallows, picking up large, black spiny sea urchins. At each catch, they stopped, sat together on an exposed rock, broke open the shell, and ate the sea urchins raw on the spot. They did not smile, and they talked little. But their eyes were tight with pleasure. They moved with a simple grace and ease, and seemed as much a part of the setting as the graceful coco palms and the solemn sea turtles. They were living creatures, turning sea into flesh and will and contentment. But for the colorful, cotton clothes, they might have been doing this two hundred years ago.

Wetlands such as this reef are, because of their richness and diversity, the best places to hunt, trap, or gather food. Walk through a northern forest and you'll notice that, as you climb up the ridges from the river valleys, the number of plant and animal species diminishes. A forest of lodgepole pine is silent, for few insects live on lodgepoles and few birds nest in them. But downslope in the river valleys are willow, alder, gooseberry and currant, shooting star and columbine. There are dragonflies, gnats, craneflies, mosquitoes, and clouds of mayflies swarming over the quiet pools. Half a dozen species of warbler and vireo feed in the willows. Sandpipers nest on the gravel bars, and kingfishers wait in snags over the water for small fish. Lowland flood plains have even greater richness and diversity. That is where trappers today ply their craft. That is where most of our duck hunting clubs are. And the movement of tides into and out of coastal marshes and tide flats brings into bay waters nutrients that feed shellfish and juvenile salmon and herring. These edges are still favorite gathering places for people who take their food directly from nature.

Most of the world's surviving subsistence cultures are wetland cultures. Eskimos, for example, are a wetland people. Sixty percent of the food taken by the Yupik Eskimos of the Yukon-Kuskokwim Delta in Alaska is food they have hunted, gathered, or fished in wet places. All summer they catch salmon, and smoke and dry them. To this winter larder, they add berries, which are gathered along the rivers,

Ruby Marsh, Nevada

dried, and mixed with animal fat. By the time spring rolls around, they may be extremely low on stored supplies, and they eagerly await the first northering flocks of geese. If the ice goes out early enough, their first fresh spring food will be seal meat. In the end of summer, they hunt geese and ducks, which are molting wingfeathers and are, therefore, flightless. "We go moose hunting and rabbit hunting and ptarmigan hunting," says Barbara Anvil, a Yupik woman who spends her summers putting up fish at her camp on the Kuskokwim River near Bethel. "Our main food is what we get ourselves."

Anvil is surrounded by drying frames of peeled cottonwood, on which hang hundreds of blood red salmon. The fish are filleted and spread open with pins of willow. It is said that you can tell where an Eskimo is from by the style in which the drying fish are thus butterflied. Each summer, Anvil puts up four to five hundred fish, and each fish weighs ten to fifteen pounds. Mat Bean, another Eskimo, says when he was a boy his family put up thirty thousand chum salmon a year to keep the dogs fed through winter. "Now we don't put up as much fish as we used to because the snow machines have replaced the dogs," he says.

Anvil's occupation and her outlook are echoed all up and down the Pacific flyway by peoples who still derive much of their food from the land. To the south and east, Indians of the northern forest also depend upon wetlands for subsistence. They rely much upon fish taken from the rivers in summer. In late summer, they hunt flightless ducks on the molting lakes. In winter, they trap mink, muskrat, beaver, and otter through holes in the ice. They snare snowshoe hares on the willow banks in winter. When the Cree and Ojibway go moose hunting, they go out by boat or canoe to look for moose in streamside willow thickets. Moose are adapted especially to feeding on aquatic plants, like water lilies, burreed and duck potato, and are seldom found far from water.

Indians of the northwest Pacific coast also derive much of their living in the wetlands, fishing the rivers and estuaries, gathering aquatic plants and shellfish. In the past, the richness of their wetland environment gave them some of the most densely settled and complex cultures of pre-conquest America. They lived in villages of more than one thousand inhabitants and had hereditary castes of noblemen and slaves and specialists in various kinds of hunting and fishing. Salmon entered the coastal rivers and moved upstream by the tens of thousands. Waterfowl visited the marshes in similar numbers. The Indians hunted sea lions and whales. When weather kept them off the ocean, they dug clams, gathered mussels and tubers and berries, or simply ate the dried fish they had stored. The fish oil in their diets compensated for the lack of carbohydrates in the plant foods offered by the dense conifer forest around them. The techniques of wetland foraging were varied and detailed. Today, Tlingit Indians of coastal Alaska still put spruce branches in the surf when the herring come in to spawn. The branches catch the sticky herring eggs, and the Indians gather the branches and snack on the roe.

California Indians had the densest populations of any pre-conquest American peoples, and did so only because their wetland environment was so rich. Around San Francisco Bay, there are hundreds of shell mounds, the rubbish heaps and old living floors of centuries of Indian settlement. Some mounds are twenty feet high and half a mile wide. Early California farmers found that after they harvested their crops, some of the hillocks in their fields had a bluish tinge, the result of mussel shells discarded there by Indians. The mounds contained clams and mussels for the most part, but in places near the coast, there were remains of abalone and cockleshell. And mixed with the shellfish remains were the bones of deer, tule elk, beaver, bear, seal, sea lion, whale, porpoise, egret, duck, goose, and turtle.

South of California, along the coast of the Gulf of California, survives one of the last hunting-gathering peoples of the earth. The Seri Indians in historic times depended upon fish from the ocean for half their food and on green sea turtles for perhaps another 25 percent. When Europeans first saw them, the Seri wore skirts of pelican skin and ate both eelgrass and the black brant that wintered in the eelgrass beds off Tiburon Island. They kept no food in storage. If fish were not running or if the geese hadn't arrived for winter, there were clams and mussels to collect in the tide flats and crabs to harvest among the mangroves.

Subsistence cultures were wetland cultures even in unlikely places. In the Nevada desert, archaeologists are finding Indian burials that contain fishhooks of bird bone, robes of coot skin, arrows fletched with pelican feathers, and ropes, baskets, and duck decoys made of tule reeds. The Piute Indians of western Nevada were a desert people who lived by fishing, waterfowling, and digging the roots of cattail—a people more devoted to the flexibility of tule than to the concussiveness of flint. Ninety percent of the food of the Indians of Pyramid Lake, northeast of Reno, came from the lake and the neighboring marshes.

The evidence of surviving subsistence cultures and of the paleontologic record for hundreds of thousands of years suggests strongly that humankind evolved in wetlands. The oldest human remains are found in the river valleys of East Africa, along with the bones of hippopotamus and other water-dependent creatures. While we make much of the surviving stone axes and spears, and think of prehistoric peoples as children of a bludgeon culture, our ancestors might well have belonged instead to reed cultures and been much gentler and more considerate than our archaeology makes them out to be. Rushwork does not fossilize as the axes do. Much evidence does not survive. But there are suggestions that life near water shaped human form and outlook.

British marine biologist Alister Hardy once argued that humankind evolved in an aquatic habitat, most likely the seacoast. He held that such an origin would explain the species' loss of body hair, the fact that humans alone among primates have the subcutaneous fat that marine mammals have, and the fact that human body hair is arranged in patterns that suggest streamlining to aid in swimming. He said that an aquatic origin would also help explain the peculiar human need for iodine and salt, the human inclination to high-protein intake, and the apparent benefits humans get from unsaturated fats. It might also explain how babies can be taught to swim at a few weeks of age. Our erect posture might even be explained as an adaptation to wading deep into water.

The more recent history of humankind is clearer. Human society is seldom found far from water. We live near rivers, not just because we need the water to drink. The wetlands of river valleys and seacoasts are the most productive lands on earth. Ecologist Eugene Odum has shown that salt marshes in Georgia produce twenty times more biomass than the open ocean. Georgia salt marshes can produce twice as much organic matter per acre as our most productive

Pacific white-fronted and cackling Canada geese, Sacramento Valley, California

hayfields. Connecticut marshes yield three hundred pounds of scallops per acre, far more than most pastures produce in beef. Ponds in Asia produce one thousand pounds of shrimp and two thousand pounds of fish per acre per year. And the areas associated with rivers, the floodplains and estuaries, receive much of the productivity of the land in flood season and so become nurseries for salmon and herring and other fish. We have always availed ourselves of that bounty.

We tend today to think of hunting-and-gathering peoples as being creatures of the plains and mountains. We have typed them in the mold of our plains Indians or of the mountain hunters of South America, largely because these are the people we encountered last and studied most. The Indian cultures of the eastern U.S. were wetland cultures, but were often ravaged by conquest or European disease before they were much studied. In South America, the dominant peoples were riverine village dwellers who grew root crops, fished, and hunted aquatic mammals and reptiles. The silt-laden waters of annual floods rejuvenated their soils. European diseases decimated these people before Europeans much realized what the natives were like. We studied instead the hunters who survived in the hinterlands. But anthropologist Donald Lathrap observes, "Most of the primitive groups inhabiting the tropical forest uplands away from the major flood plains can be interpreted as the wreckage of evolved agricultural societies forced into an environment unsuitable to the basic economic pattern. Deprived of the riverine resources (by competition with other groups), such groups had to rely on the hunting of forest game to provide the protein and fat essential to the diet."

Wetlands must once have been the central focus of human thought and activity. Anthropologist Irving Goldman observed of the Cubeo of the northwest Amazon, "The river is the most important territory. It is a highway and a link between related sibs, the source of ancestral power, and the economic zone of men, fish being the main source of animal protein. Even most land animals are hunted along the river banks. The orientation of the Cubeo is toward the river and not toward the forest. The river is the source of the ancestral powers . . . the forest is a source

mainly of dangers." The example of the Cubeo might stand for all humankind centuries ago. In primitive religious mythology, water is a central image. The deities associated with rivers—frogs in Central America or pythons in Africa—are creatures of insight, wisdom, and patience.

We still have dim memories of such a world in our own modern religions. The Garden of Eden was watered by four rivers that rose from the Tree of Life. A prayer to the Sumerian goddess Engur addresses her as "Thou river, creator of all things." The Egyptian goddess Mut, or "watery one," was mother of all things. The presiding deities of the Ganges, the Indus, and the Niger were all mother goddesses. Anahita, the Zoroastrian goddess of springs and rivers, presided over childbirth and nurturing until, carried abroad by Persian armies, she lost her riparian pedigree and became Aphrodite, goddess of love.

Clearly, living by water for hundreds of thousands of years has shaped our human outlook. We universally regard water as cleansing and restful. We universally regard the sound of water as musical, while the sound of rustling leaves or morning birdsong may not strike us as pleasant. We universally believe a landscape is more attractive if there is water in view, not water locked in ice or snow or passing by in clouds—not the potential of water, but the actuality, glancing blue at the sky, tossing off glints of sunlight, surging, restless, leaping, alive.

Living by water doubtless also nurtured human curiosity. Rivers and swamps and seacoasts give us objects of fascination. They bring us shells, the carapaces of turtles, strange beach-tossed carcasses suggestive of sea monsters and fallen gods, bits of beach vine and kelp, driftwood and oddly shaped pebbles, puzzles urging us to think on the broader nature of things. Simply to think about the provenance of fish and clam and unseen creatures in the mud is to think beyond the reach of the eye. We all today still have a wetland curiosity, the childhood fascination of walking along a rocky river bed or a storm-littered beach, looking for curiosity and art, finding strange textures and shapes, filling our pockets with brightly colored stones or seashells.

And while scenes like that on the reef at Kealakekua Bay grow increasingly rare, while we live increas-

ingly in cities, while our rivers become bone-white concrete channels, our lakes become parking lots of asphalt, and water hides behind pipes and tap handles, we still have a wetland curiosity and a reverence for water. Wetlands tug at our minds when we drive over a bridge and catch the glint of water below. They call to us in the sound of sea waves or the sight of geese flying high on an autumn evening. What we may be seeing in the passage of goose or sandpiper over the wet places of the earth are tracks in the sky of our own human wanderings.

Snow geese, Tule Lake, Klamath Basin, California

Flathead River Valley, Montana

Lesser sandhill cranes, Carrizo Plains, California

American avocet, Malheur Basin, Oregon

Pacific white-fronted geese, Tule Lake, Klamath Basin, California

White pelican young, Tule Lake, Klamath Basin, California

Tule elk, San Joaquin Valley, California

Rocky Mountain Trench, Columbia River, British Columbia

White pelicans, Red Rock Lakes, Montana

Cinnamon teal, Malheur Basin, Oregon

Greater sandhill crane, nest & young, Malheur Basin, Oregon

Dowitchers, Flathead River Valley, Montana

Sacramento Valley, California

Wood ducks, Sacramento Valley, California

Hooded mergansers, Rocky Mountain Trench, Columbia River, British Columbia, Canada

Brooks, Alberta, is the heart of the prairie pothole country. The rolling plains spread in all directions. In April, the treeless countryside is the color of gray sage and winter-killed grass. The sky is so clear you can see a hundred miles. No distant mountain ridges stop the seepage of the imagination. The landscape's monuments are apt to be water tanks and pronghorn antelopes. In most years, April still sees snow on the ground. But there has been a drought in southern Alberta for three years. January was so summery that people wore shorts on the streets of Brooks. There has been no rain. The potholes are drying out. And that's bad news to American duck hunters. For, 10 percent of the continent's nesting habitat—the pothole country of Alberta, Saskatchewan, Manitoba, and the Dakotas—produces something like 60 percent of the continent's ducks. As the potholes dry out, the ducks vanish. In 1970, more than ten million ducks wintered in California, most of them Canadian-bred. In 1984, only two million wintered there.

A pothole is a depression in the glaciated ground, into which snowmelt and groundwater gather each spring and summer. The ponds fill with bullrush, pondweed, spikerush, and dozens of other plants that feed ducks. A single pothole outside the Brooks Wildlife Center, surrounded by grazing cattle, has already this April attracted two nesting pairs of pintail, a pair of mallard, a pair of shovelers, and a pair of Canada geese. Summers tend to dry the potholes out. Early in the season, the ducks spend a lot of time flying up, circling over the countryside, and landing again on the pothole. Ed Hoffman, a biologist with the Alberta Division of Fish and Wildlife, believes these scouting flights are made to learn where the neighboring potholes are, so that if the brood pond dries out, a duck may lead its young overland to a surviving pond. Ducks may also require several potholes to bring off a brood, each pothole providing different food resources to meet the changing nutritional needs of young ducks.

Every year, the Canadian Wildlife Service flies transects over southern Alberta, counting potholes to predict nesting activity. The aerial surveys show the numbers of potholes have declined. In May of 1984, there were only about two-thirds the number of an average year, and by July, half of them were gone. In 1985, after a wet fall, pond numbers rose 50 percent. But the duck yield didn't rise correspondingly. Mallard production went up only 4 percent. Says Bruce Turner of the Canadian Wildlife Service, "There's habitat out there that's not being occupied." And the nesting success in occupied habitat is only about 9 percent. Says Hoffman, "It's been said that you have to have a nesting success rate of 15 percent to maintain the population." Most biologists think the reduced number of potholes has concentrated coyotes and foxes around the remaining ponds, and that accounts for the low success.

The drought will pass, but its consequences may not. If you look around Brooks, you'll see that the prairie is vanishing. On both sides of the road leading to the Brooks Wildlife Center, there are freshly plowed fields. "Two years ago on both sides of the road were native prairie," says Hoffman. Farmers are encouraged to plow up more ground because they sell to government grain commissions, which set purchase quotas on the basis of the acreage a farmer cultivates. The more ground a farmer plows, the more he gets from the commission. And the lowered water table of the drought makes it easier to level and fill potholes. "Every year that goes by when potholes don't have any water, that allows the farmer to cultivate more of them," says Hoffman. "The little two- to three-acre potholes are the real mainstays for waterfowl. Unfortunately, that is what's disappearing at such an alarming rate. If we do get a wet year, these potholes won't be available for nesting." Hoffman estimates that southern Alberta is losing habitat at a rate of 2 percent per year. "You spread that out over ten or fifteen years and it's a lot." Things have already gone so far," he says, that "if we could save all the habitat

Tule Lake, Klamath Basin, California

that's out there today, and not do anything to improve it, we'd still be on a downhill trend."

Neither the Canadian nor the provincial governments spend money to improve waterfowl habitat. Canada has no national wildlife refuge system comparable to the United States', and the provinces have only begun to operate wetland breeding areas. Canadians don't have the big winter waterfowl concentrations the U.S. has. The first October blizzard sends the ducks south, and with them goes the political constituency that might organize a Canadian refuge system. Since the 1930s, when Americans discovered that habitat protection was as important as season and bag limits in conserving waterfowl, U.S. hunters have funnelled millions of dollars a year into the Canadian pothole country through Ducks Unlimited (DU). DU pays landowners to sign twenty-one-year agreements to flood land and manage it as wetlands. The agreement benefits the farmer as much as it benefits the hunter. Much of southern Alberta is overgrazed. In drought years, the overgrazed land simply blows away on the wind. Motorists in Brooks sometimes drive at midday with headlights on because of the blowing dust. Some ranges have lost the entire A horizon of topsoil. The cattle cluster near water. By developing water tanks and potholes around the countryside, DU projects spread the cattle out and reduce erosion.

So far, DU projects have protected more than 3.6 million acres of Canadian wetlands. In the 24-square-mile Kitsim Project, just west of Brooks, DU built a 150-acre reservoir and pumped water into sixty-nine potholes. Jay Bartsch, DU's area manager in Brooks, estimates the project has increased the carrying capacity of the range 20 percent, and will produce fourteen thousand ducks a year on lands that had ceased to breed waterfowl. With such projects, says Bartsch, "DU probably controls more breeding habitat now than there is native habitat. If we get some wet years back to back, we'd get the duck populations back."

It is hard to say whether Bartsch or Hoffman is right, whether we'll ever see ten million ducks wintering again in California. But it is clear that our traditional preoccupation with prairie potholes and breeding grounds in Canada may leave us shortsighted. The more serious problem in the flyway today may be the wintering grounds in California and other western states.

On a November evening, John Cowan likes to stand in the marsh on the sunset side of California's Gray Lodge Waterfowl Management Area and watch one of the great spectacles of American wildlife. Through clumps of tule and rush, Cowan can see clusters of pintails and wigeons and lines of elegant white snow geese on the water. There is the sound of splashing as masses of ducks and geese preen and wash. Over the rush of water come the cries of geese, the nasal cranks of mallards, the whistles of pintails, and the squeaky exclamations of wigeons. It is impossible from the noise to tell how many thousands of birds are crammed into this marsh.

Minutes after the sun goes down, however, there is a sudden roar, like the sound of a jet aircraft taking off. From the marsh rise twenty or thirty thousand snow geese. The white of their wings flashes pink in the glow of the sunset. The roar of wingbeats gives way to a din of high-pitched whoops, which build into a roar like that of a cheering crowd in a football stadium. The geese circle, tossing the sunlight, sideslipping on the wind, and return to the marsh. Smaller groups take off and circle, as if urging the mass to join them. As the sky darkens, the ducks, too, begin to rise in groups of two or five or twelve. Wigeons whistle overhead. Pintails fly so low that one can hear the wind lisping through gaps between wingfeathers. As the twilight grows murky, the shapes loom out of the marsh like bats. They rise and break apart, clusters of them, then waves, then clouds. The rush of wings and the din of squawk and whistle fill the air. The birds boil up out of the marsh, now by the hundreds, now by the thousands. Within twenty minutes, there are nearly one million birds in the air.

It is lavish abundance. It is the lively energy of large birds, clean against the rising moon, full of will and purpose. "Seeing that evening flight is just the greatest thrill," says Cowan, who for thirty years was the manager of Gray Lodge. Today, he watches the night flight and thinks about how things must once have been. California's Central Valley, the broad plain between the Coast Range and the Sierra Nevada, was once four million acres of wetland. The rivers flooded in winter and spread out over the valley floor in lakes and swamps and inland seas. All that water spawned aquatic plants and invertebrates, which, in turn, drew wintering ducks and geese and shorebirds in unimaginable numbers. Early settlers said flocks blackened the skies. They said geese covered the ground completely for miles at a stretch. In the 1890s, Dr. Hugh Glenn employed twenty to forty goose herders at a time on his Sacramento Valley wheat farms to shoot geese out of his fields. He spent thirteen thousand dollars a year just supplying them with ammunition.

Today, such spectacles as Gray Lodge's night flight are rare. You see them at Gray Lodge during the hunting season because the birds have crowded into this refuge to escape the guns of hunters. At dusk, when hunters must stop hunting, the birds fly off to feed in neighboring grain fields. Over most of the state, the great flocks of waterfowl are gone. They have gone because the wetlands have gone.

Most of California is arid, and to lubricate fields and factories and keep dust off its suburban streets, California has sponged up water wherever it ponds, funnelled it into ditches and canals, and husbanded it narrowly to human purposes. California once boasted over five million acres of wetlands; 91 percent of that is gone. In San Francisco Bay, 75 percent of the wetlands, including 95 percent of its original marshes, have vanished. Of the marshes along the south coast, 75 percent have been filled. Of the original four million acres of Central Valley wetlands, 96 percent are gone. Tulare Lake, once a vast sea in winter, is today planted almost entirely in cotton. Most of the original great blue heron rookeries in the valley are gone. There were once white pelican colonies all up and down the valley; today there are none. The tule elk, a small, swamp-loving species, today survives only on refuges.

"If you look back over the last thirty years," says Cowan, "the destruction of habitat in the Sacramento Valley has been very discouraging." As a boy, Cowan hunted the bypasses and tule marshes of the valley. "There were swales," he says. "There were potholes. The birds had a lot of places to go." Today, the Sacramento River and its tributary creeks have been corseted in levees. The trees have been torn from the bottom lands to make room for crops. The farm lands have been leveled with laser-guided tractors. They are so flat that rainwater finds no place to pond. The fields come right down to the edge of the river.

Tundra swans, Butte Sink, Sacramento Valley, California

Habitat for wintering birds is perilously small. "I can take you up in an airplane and show you in a couple of hours the entire wintering habitat," says Daniel Connelly of the California Department of Fish and Game. In the Central Valley, it is compressed into 80,000 acres of state and federal refuges and wildlife management areas and about 300,000 acres of private lands, most of which are duck hunting clubs. Half the duck clubs are rice farms that flood fields after harvest and lease them out to hunters. Here and there, as in the Butte Sink or the Grasslands near Los Banos, there are organized duck clubs, which plant rice to attract ducks. The Sacramento Valley has over 500,000 acres of rice fields, which provide stubble fields for the birds to feed on in the fall. But as foreign competition pushed California rice farming into a depression, the fields have increasingly converted to almond and pistachio orchards, which offer nothing to wintering birds. And as the owners of hunt clubs age, younger hunters can't meet the inflated price of the land and management, so duck clubs have sold out, returned to agriculture or become industrial parks.

Further loss of California's wetlands can have far-reaching effects. California winters 60 percent of the ducks and geese of the Pacific flyway, one-fifth of the entire continent's waterfowl population. The Central Valley alone hosts half the flyway's pintail and wigeon, 80 percent of the shovelers, 60 percent of the gadwalls, 82 percent of the snow geese, and 86 percent of the tundra swans. Some species—such as the cackling Canada goose, Ross' goose, and the Aleutian Canada goose—winter only in the Central Valley. And it's not only ducks that might suffer from further losses. As the wetlands go, so will go the phalaropes, the grebes, the sandpipers, the egrets, the herons, and the rails. So, too, will go the fisheries. The Sacramento-San Joaquin Delta once hosted a dozen fish canneries and thriving commercial fisheries in salmon, shad, perch, and sturgeon. Today the canneries are gone and the delta has only sport fisheries. Striped bass populations in San Francisco Bay are 10 percent of what they were in 1970. Salmon fishermen from San Francisco must now fish in Oregon and Washington waters for Columbia River stocks.

It's not just a question of quantity, either. The quality of the remaining wetlands is also declining.

During the hunting season, from October to January, the birds squeeze into small sanctuary zones on the refuges to escape hunters. Crowding encourages epidemics of botulism and avian cholera. At times, refuge personnel must go out and stack corpses like cordwood and burn them. The concentration also adds to the considerable stress of wintering in an urban state. Hunting is part of that stress. As the season wears on, hunter bags show a declining number of young birds and an increasing proportion of adults, showing that the harvest cuts into the breeding stock. There is heavy human activity in and around the wintering grounds. Airplanes and helicopters whine overhead. Says Mark Strong, wildlife biologist at the Sacramento National Wildlife Refuge, "A helicopter coming over at legal altitudes will put every goose in the air." Sightseers and birdwatchers driving through the refuges also put birds to flight. Studies by Michael Miller of the U.S. Fish and Wildlife Service and Daniel Connelly and John Beam of the California Department of Fish and Game show that pintails, green-winged teals, and shovelers in the Central Valley lose weight between October and January.

A serious adversity is the change in food offered the wintering birds. "Forty years ago," says Ed Collins, manager of the Sacramento National Wildlife Refuge, "there was enough choice out there that the birds could go out and choose what they needed." But with the conversion to farmland and channelization of the rivers, the choices have thinned out. There are no natural wetlands left in the valley. All the remaining ponds are managed, fed by ditches and canals, rather than by floods. "Over 80 percent of the plants in the valley are now non-native," says Cowan. "Just fields of star thistle and stuff like that. I'm sure ducks can't use that. We have developed a monoculture of rice fields, and you don't have the diversity of aquatic plants that grow in those potholes and riparian habitat."

Rice fields are considered a boon to waterfowl. The refuges of the Sacramento Valley were established in part to relieve farmers of crop damage by providing ducks and geese with their own rice fields. Farmers now use earlier maturing varieties of rice, and the ducks and geese now stop to feed in grain fields planted at the Klamath Basin refuges to the north and so arrive later in the fall. So crop depredation is not

the problem it once was. Still, the birds feed in the rice stubble after harvest, and duck clubs continue to plant rice to attract ducks.

But rice is not enough. At the Sacramento National Wildlife Refuge, biologists Mickey Heitmeier and Dennis Ravelling have been looking at what ducks eat to get through winter. Between September and March, the birds must fuel their bodies through the pre-alternate molt, which gives pintails their long tails and mallards their green heads, then courtship and a pre-basic molt, which gives the hens their camouflage plumage, and then they must fatten up for the northward migration. Each of these tasks requires its own nutritional strategy, and the ducks therefore change their feeding behavior several times during winter. Wigeon, for example, feed on submerged plants in October, then switch to moist soil seeds and rootstocks, and then, late in winter, switch again to feeding on grasses in upland areas. Mallards eat moist soil seeds in the fall, switch in midwinter to high-energy foods like acorns or row crops, and later move on to a diet of invertebrates. "What we're finding out," says Heitmeier, "is that birds don't just eat one thing in winter. They eat a whole bunch of things. They eat one thing when they lay an egg and a different thing when they brood an egg. It's important that they get the right resource at the right time." If they don't get enough protein to complete the molt, courtship will be delayed. If courtship is late, migration is late. The later the bird returns north, the less likely it is to fledge young.

To complete its molt, a bird needs protein. "Row crops provide a lot of energy," says Heitmeier. But ducks can't assimilate protein from row crops. They get protein from moist soil seeds and invertebrates. Mallards, Heitmeier calculates, need five to ten grams of protein a day to get through a molt. "Say they only get half that per day: they can take the needed protein out of their muscle mass, or they can delay the molt." One recourse will weaken the bird and make it more vulnerable to predators. The other will delay migration and reduce the bird's chances of breeding.

The biologists conclude that natural marshes are essential to the birds. "We think the birds are adapted to these marshes historically," says Heitmeier. "Since we've changed the marshes so much, we wonder what we've done to the nutrition of the birds." Most

Tule Lake, Klamath Basin, California

of the remaining wetlands are flooded only in the hunting season and therefore don't grow the moist soil plants and invertebrates that ducks require. "Most of our duck clubs are loafing and resting areas," says Cowan. "They don't provide very much feed." On top of that, says Strong, "The clubs just pull their boards and drain their ponds as soon as hunting season is over. They just go home and don't want to think about it again until the fall." Strong spends much of his time trying to convince duck-club owners to manage for natural wetlands. But not all duck clubs want to pay the cost of year-round water management. Cowan urges the state and federal refuges to keep at least 10 percent of their area in permanent ponds, but even they fail to meet this quota. Permanent water is hard to find in this valley.

Even the short-season ponds on the duck clubs may be in trouble. As fewer ducks come down the flyway, the hunting season is shortened to reduce the hunters' take, and the hunt-club fields are drained even earlier. Moreover, as fewer ducks come down the flyway and hunters have a harder time filling their bags, the number of duck hunters declines. In 1970, there were 1.5 million ducks harvested in California by 188,876 hunters. In 1980, 625,000 ducks were harvested by 108,753 hunters. By 1986, there were only 92,753 hunters. As the hunters decline, the number of duck clubs declines. Between 1983 and 1985, the number of duck clubs on San Francisco Bay dropped from twelve to five. Duck clubs in the Sacramento Delta are sold to become industrial parks and farms. Each year, more private wetlands are dried out. Each year, the fate of the migrants rests heavier on the ability of state and federal refuges to provide.

But the refuges have problems of their own. Sixty-six percent of the water delivered to the nine federal refuges in the Central Valley is provided by the Bureau of Reclamation from the Central Valley Project on an "if and when available" basis. The refuges have no legal rights to that water. The bureau doesn't recognize wildlife as a beneficial use of project water and will not bind itself to contracts for delivery. Kern and Pixley national wildlife refuges in the southern San Joaquin have rights to no water. Kern floods only 2,500 of its 10,000 acres. San Luis National Wildlife

Refuge needs 19,000 acre-feet of water a year, but has rights to only 3,500. Sacramento, Delevan, and Colusa refuges in the Sacramento Valley have been getting 105,000 acre-feet a year at the pleasure of the Bureau of Reclamation, but have no contractual rights to any of it. Demand for water is growing in California at a rate of 1 percent per year, but new supplies are unlikely to be developed because farmers can't pay the $400- to $500-per-acre-foot cost of newly developed water, and the public no longer wants to subsidize farmers. As demand increases, the bureau could award the water now going to refuges to the farmers.

Water conservation might make more water available to the refuges. But it would come at the cost of water to the private wetlands, most of which flood their fields with agricultural return flows, water that has already passed through fields. Rice farmers have reduced their water consumption about 20 percent, but that means less water may go to the duck clubs.

The refuges depend heavily on the ability to manipulate what water they get. To manage for native vegetation, they must flood and drain ponds several times a year. Marsh vegetation in the west is adapted to cycles of drying out and flooding. Flooding is also the most effective means of keeping tules and other weeds from choking out the ponds. But the refuges depend upon irrigation districts to conduct the federal water to their ponds. And because they get water on an "if and when available" basis, they get it only when the irrigation districts have the capacity to deliver it. Says Strong, "When we are first starting to put water on the ground for the rice crops, that's when all the farmers are putting water on their rice fields. We're at the end of the ditch. We have to wait our turn in line."

Sometimes the turn doesn't come in time. In 1985, Gary Zahm, manager of the Kesterson, Merced, and San Luis refuges near Los Banos, asked the irrigation district to deliver water needed for a germinating millet crop. The company told him it would be ten to twelve days before he could have the water, and while he waited, the crop simply dried up. At times, Zahm has had to borrow water from neighboring farmers who are higher on the district's priority list. Things get even harder in winter when the birds are in the

refuges. The irrigation districts shut down their reservoirs and canals in November for maintenance work. "Between December 1 and February 1," says Zahm, "although there is fresh water available for the refuge, I can't get it."

The refuges don't have their own delivery systems. They used to pump water from their own deep wells, but today the energy cost is too high. San Luis Refuge pays seventy-eight cents an acre-foot for water delivered through the irrigation district's gravity flow canal. It costs eleven to sixteen dollars to pump an acre-foot of water from the refuge's own wells. Cuts in refuge funding simply don't allow the refuges to spend that kind of money. "We've taken some of these wetlands out of production mainly because we couldn't afford to do it anymore," says Zahm. For example, the Merced Refuge spent $46,000 to flood 1,000 acres in 1976. In 1982 it spent $55,000 to flood only 590 acres. In 1983, it flooded only 320 acres.

The state waterfowl management areas have the same problem. To save water at the Los Banos Waterfowl Management Area, the managers grow swamp timothy instead of watergrass, even though the birds are thought to rely on watergrass in December and January because it provides the carbohydrates they need to get through the cold winter months. Gray Lodge has been flooding its fields later in the year and, in consequence, producing less food. At Honey Lake Waterfowl Management Area, managers have stopped pumping water in the fall and have started to manage chiefly for spring nesting populations instead.

If water quantity is a problem, water quality may prove a disaster. All the Central Valley refuges and most of the duck clubs rely on agricultural waste water to flood their fields. It is water that has run through farm fields and collected in drains and ditches. Often, it carries loads of salts, pesticides, and toxic chemicals.

In 1965, the Bureau of Reclamation began to deliver Central Valley Project water to new farmlands west of Fresno. Much of the land there was underlain by impervious clay barriers, which kept irrigation water from dribbling down to the water table and caused it to puddle under the fields like water in a

Bald eagle, Tule Lake, Klamath Basin, California

shrinking. As it shrinks, it gets saltier. It is already saltier than seawater, and eventually it will be too salty to support the fish, the invertebrates, and most of the birds.

Both the U.S. Fish and Wildlife Service and the State of California have long been aware that California's wetlands are disappearing. But they have been unable to find ways to stop the trend. The state pledged in 1952 to provide more adequate waterfowl habitat, bought four parcels and ran out of money. In 1964, a state Wetlands Task Force recommended more purchases, but the legislature voted no funds. In 1966, the California Fish and Wildlife Plan urged more purchases, but again there was no funding.

The Fish and Wildlife Service has been interested chiefly in waterfowl because hunters' duck stamps are the principle source of funds with which to acquire habitat. The service is trying to buy up easements on forty-nine thousand acres of duck habitat in the Central Valley, most of it in the Butte Sink and the Grasslands area. The easements would bind duck clubs or farmers to flood their fields through most of the winter. But farmers won't sell easements, lest they reduce the borrowing value of the land. Duck clubs are really the only takers. And the program doesn't address the water delivery or water quality problems that beset the refuges. Since 1983, the service has sought to have wildlife named a beneficial use of the Bureau of Reclamation's water and to secure rights to at least some portion of the 550,000 acre-feet needed to manage the state and federal waterfowl areas in California. Though the Bureau of Reclamation has one million acre-feet of unappropriated water, it has opposed the petition.

In 1979, the California legislature directed the Department of Fish and Game to come up with a plan to protect all the state's remaining wetlands and, by purchase or easement, add 50 percent to the existing total. The plan was written, some funds were made available from the state's Wildlife Conservation Fund, and, in 1984, voters approved an $85 million bond measure aimed at saving wetlands. But the money doesn't come close to the $481 million price tag the department put on the 1979 goal.

Meanwhile as state spending on existing programs declines, California does a poorer job of managing the wetlands it already has. Staff cutbacks have left the Department of Fish and Game unable to manage its own waterfowl management areas. At the Imperial Wildlife Management Area on the Salton Sea, the maintenance crew has been cut from ten to five, and manager Chris Gonzales worries now that cattails "are going to take over a lot of our habitat." At Honey Lake Wildlife Management Area, the staff has been cut 40 percent. Says area manager Kit Novick, "Right now we have a number of lands which are idle because we don't have the manpower." The budget for the Los Banos Wildlife Management Area has been cut 25 percent over the last three years. A newly acquired 17,000-acre area in the Butte Valley near Klamath Lake has a staff of one. Another acquisition in Ash Valley has no manager.

Private organizations have stepped in to help. The California Waterfowl Association, seeing that the state could not conduct some necessary research, hired its own biologist and started a "high density nesting project" at the state's Grizzly Island Wildlife Management Area in Suisun Marsh. The association's biologist, Bob McLandress, found that mallards were nesting at Grizzly Island in densities ten times those found in healthy Canadian pothole habitat. The project now aims to improve water management at Grizzly Island—and possibly other state waterfowl management areas—to increase the number of breeding mallards, in part to make up for the decline of Canadian-bred pintails. The Nature Conservancy and the National Audubon Society have both made efforts to purchase critical wetlands in California. The Nature Conservancy already has projects underway in the Coachella Valley near the Salton Sea, on the Cosumnes River on the edge of the Central Valley, and on the Carrizo Plain, a large soda lake that hosts large numbers of wintering sandhill cranes in San Luis Obispo County. The Audubon Society has been negotiating for purchase of valuable Central Valley wetlands near Modesto. However, even combined with state and federal activities, these efforts don't stop the overall loss of wetlands.

No one expects this trend to reverse itself. Says Strong, "The long-term trend is way down. There's no question but there will be a continuing trend to convert more wetlands into croplands. We're fighting for every acre here. But I think we've already lost so much that we can't take care of the waterfowl populations we once had."

What is happening in California is happening all over the west. It is especially intense in the arid states, where most of the wetlands are along the rivers that humankind harnesses to novel purposes. In Arizona, the state's major rivers have all been dammed, channelized, and diverted to provide water for farms and fast-growing cities. As a result, says David Brown of the Arizona Department of Game and Fish, "The riverine wetlands, the backwaters, have really taken a beating. Ninety to 95 percent of them have been destroyed." Those in the south central part of the state were gone by 1915. Completion of Boulder Dam in 1935 brought flood controls that sent developers scurrying to fill the old marshes along the lower Colorado. Filling, dredging, and straightening the river below Boulder Dam so reduced habitat that by 1980, more than 80 percent of what remained was in the two national wildlife refuges, Imperial and Cibola. In 1988, when the Central Arizona Project is fully operating, it will dewater most of the lower Colorado. With the loss of natural wetlands, Arizona's stock ponds, storage reservoirs, and sewage treatment lagoons have become significant wetlands. But around the storage reservoirs, the shorelines fluctuate so greatly that vegetation doesn't get established. The reservoirs are chiefly useful to birds as loafing ponds as they pass through.

Most of Arizona's remaining wetlands are now in the meadows and marshes of the mountains of the north of the state, where impermeable subsoils trap snowmelt and rainwater and hold it into the dry months of summer. Many of these ponds have been modified by ranchers and recreation developers to increase storage or to invite summer-home development. But the fluctuating shorelines and the wake of powerboats limit their productivity. Ultimately, says Brown, "A pristine wetland marsh in Arizona is going to be at a premium."

In Wyoming and Idaho, the same trends are evident. Less than 5 percent of Wyoming is wetland, but

Trumpeter swan, Red Rock Lakes, Montana

that fraction supports more than 20 percent of the state's wild species and makes Wyoming the nation's sixth leading producer of waterfowl. According to Dave Lockman, migratory bird biologist for the Wyoming Department of Game and Fish, "We're losing more than we can gain." Most people in Wyoming think of wetlands as the prairie potholes that are increasingly plowed up by farmers in the eastern part of the state. But the rivers west of the Continental Divide are also important. The flooded bottom lands of the Green, the Salt, and the Bear, and the rivers of southern Idaho—the Blackfoot, the Snake, and the Teton—are important producers of redhead and canvasback duck and sandhill and whooping crane. They are beaver streams, thick with willows. On the Green, those willow bottoms serve as winter range for moose.

Traditionally, these rivers overflowed their banks from April to July. The floods cut oxbows and meandering channels, which stayed wet through summer. But farmers put in storage reservoirs and canals to move water at times more to their liking. In the last decade, they drained the oxbows and spirited away the overflood to increase the acreage available for pasture and haying. They cultivated right up to the stream banks, eliminating shade and cover. Cattle trampled and ate streamside willows and increased stream-bank erosion. The river then undercut the stream banks and meandered into the pasture, and the ranchers feared they were being cheated of land. So, they straightened and deepened the channels to move high water through faster. Says Lockman, "Everybody starts messing with the meander line, and the next thing you know, you've got an unstable system. You lose the stabilizing vegetation. You start getting bank cutting. And the farmer says he's losing a lot of grazing land, so he's got to straighten the thing." It's not just the river bottoms that are in trouble. In upland areas, sprinkler irrigation systems lower the groundwater that once came to the surface in semipermanent marshes. Overgrazing on the upper reaches of the streams reduces cover and increases erosion.

Lockman would like Wyoming to undertake its own inventory of wetlands. But the state officials are little aware of the seriousness of the problem. The state plans instead to phase out Lockman's job, the only official position that offers a view of wetland needs and functions statewide.

Nevada has already seen one of its federal wildlife refuges, the Winnemucca National Wildlife Refuge northeast of Reno, dry up and go out of business. It may lose another. Western Nevada was once a complex of wetlands. Ancient Lake Lahontan covered ten thousand square miles of the state fifty thousand years ago. As the climate changed, the lake receded, leaving Pyramid and Walker lakes and the seasonal marshlands of the Carson and Humboldt sinks behind. Agricultural development and diversion of the Sierra Nevada rivers in California dried much of that out. Pyramid Lake, near Reno, is the home of breeding colonies of white pelicans and Caspian terns, and the last refuge of the Lahontan cutthroat trout and the strange cui ui, a bead-eyed, tube-mouthed sucker that is the last of its genus. The lake is shrinking as agricultural and urban development divert half the flow of the Truckee River. Walker Lake, on the Carson River, is a vision of Pyramid Lake's future. Its water diverted to irrigate farmlands to the east, its shoreline is caked with alkali and its water too salty to support fish. The state's major wetlands are in the Lahontan Valley. Seventy-five percent of them have already vanished. The remaining wetlands survive by being at the end of the ditch, and being recipients of flood releases from Lahontan Reservoir, seepage from unlined irrigation canals, and waste water drained from the farms around Fallon. Efforts to force farmers to line their canals and reduce diversions from the Truckee to leave more water for the Pyramid Lake fisheries will reduce the water now going into these wetlands. The Stillwater Wildlife Management Area, a vast breeding marsh for stilts, avocets, gadwall, and cinnamon teal, is an important staging area for migrating ducks, swans, phalaropes, and sandpipers. It survives on waste water from the irrigation project. The area is jointly managed by the Nevada Fish and Game Commission and the U.S. Fish and Wildlife Service, which, in 1952, asked the Nevada state engineer for rights to unappropriated water to manage the area. The engineer has never acted on the petition. Plans to reduce the water going to farms in the Fallon area will leave Stillwater with enough water to flood only eight thousand of its twenty-nine thousand acres.

In Utah, where the state seems more committed to protecting wetlands, nature has thrown wildlife managers a curve. Instead of too little water, Utah's major wetlands have too much. Between 1982 and 1985, the Wasatch Mountains received unusually high amounts of snow and rainfall. In 1982 and 1983, rapid melting of the snow flooded creeks in Salt Lake City. In four unusually wet years, Salt Lake, which has no outlet, rose eleven feet. It flooded buildings, trailer parks, highways, railroad lines, and sewage treatment plants. The flooding has been a disaster for wildlife. In the 1930s, Civilian Conservation Corps (CCC) crews built dikes to hold fresh water back from the salt water at the mouths of the Bear, Jordan, and Weber rivers, fostering freshwater marshes that drew millions of migrating waterfowl. The eastern shore of the lake had, before the floods, 400,000 acres of freshwater marshes that accounted for more than 60 percent of Utah's wetlands. The floods devastated the marshes. Says Tom Aldrich, waterfowl coordinator for the Utah Division of Wildlife Resources, "Ninety percent of the wetlands around the Great Salt Lake are gone."

Less than 20 percent of the Ogden Bay refuge is above water. All the Bear River National Wildlife Refuge's 60,000 acres are under water. The Layton-Kaysville marsh, once 150,000 acres of mud flat hosting sandpipers, stilts, egrets, and ibis, is now under four to eight feet of water. Farmington Bay and Howard Slough are "99 percent gone."

If the lake were to stay at its current level, wildlife agencies would have to buy out lakeshore farmers to start new refuges. It would be decades before they could develop those new refuge lands. If, as expected, the lake level recedes, it will be more than a decade before the marshes already owned by state and federal agencies can be restored. At most, says Aldrich, the lake will recede one foot per year. It will take a decade to return to its 1982 level. By then, salt will have killed off the marsh plants and their seeds in the soil. The soil will be sterile.

The flooding has been hard on the migrants. Tim

White-faced ibis, dowitchers, San Luis Island, San Joaquin Valley, California

Provan, director of Utah's non-game wildlife program, fears the shorebirds and waders that migrated through Salt Lake by the millions are particularly at risk. "Five years ago," says Provan, "the lake offered an awful lot of shoreline and mud flat. The mud flats are no longer available for these birds to feed on." So avocets and stilts, egrets and herons have suffered an enormous loss of habitat. Glossy ibis, which were already seriously depleted due to exposure to DDT in Mexico, require large dense growth of hardstem bullrush, three feet above water, to breed. "We had miles and miles of that kind of vegetation," says Provan. "Now, it's totally gone." Utah once had a breeding population of 400,000 to 500,000 ibis. It was reduced by DDT to 100,000. With the nesting grounds gone, it is uncertain what will happen to the birds.

Some birds have already vanished. The Forster's and black terns that bred in colonies have gone. Ring-billed, laughing, and Bonaparte's gulls have gone. The owls and marsh hawks and eagles that once fed on fish have gone. Egrets and ibis are turning up in Cache Valley instead of Salt Lake. It is assumed by many that displaced birds will go elsewhere. The wet weather has filled desert playas to the south and west, making them potential habitat. At Clear Lake Wildlife Management Area, the lake spilled out into the desert, creating thousands of shallow-water areas. Says Aldrich, "The desert has just come alive. There's a lot of aquatic vegetation. Clear Lake is the most beautiful marsh you can imagine," sprouting salt grass, spikerush and alkali bullrush luxuriantly. It ought to appeal to waterfowl. But the birds displaced from Salt Lake aren't using it in anything like the numbers one would expect. "The majority of the birds of Utah are going elsewhere," says Aldrich. Some of the one million pintail that once visited Salt Lake in the fall are showing up at Ruby Lake, Nevada. Some authorities think the rest are going to California's Central Valley.

But no one knows. There is no clear increase in numbers elsewhere. "You would think that if one million birds were displaced, they'd show up somewhere else. They don't seem to do that," says Provan. "I don't think birds are as opportunistic as many people think. I'm convinced that all the niches are filled and

mortality takes the excess. We have to have lost millions and millions of birds."

In Washington, most of the wetlands around Seattle and Tacoma have been lost to housing and port development. Half the wetlands of Puget Sound are gone. The wetlands of the Puyallup River in Tacoma are entirely gone. At the mouth of the Green River, 640 acres of marsh have been reduced to 8, and only 55 of the original 2,500 acres of intertidal lands remain. In Commencement Bay, all 2,470 acres of wetland have been lost. Eighty-five percent of the wetlands of the Snohomish estuary are gone. Says Dave Ortman of Friends of the Earth, "The entire shoreline between Seattle and Everett is basically riprap because of the railroad, so there is no wetland there." Half the wetlands of Grays Harbor have been filled, and half the wetlands of the lower Columbia lost to dredging and disposal of dredge spoils. Ravenna Creek in Seattle is shunted through an underground pipe for 75 percent of its length, and Moxlie Creek in Olympia runs underground for more than half its length. The urban population in western Washington got the state to adopt a shoreline protection program that slows destruction of wetlands along the coast. But port development continues to threaten the coastal wetlands. And there is no halt to the loss of wetlands east of the Cascades, where farmers and ranchers drain wetlands and grazing cattle erode stream banks and remove cover on both private and public lands.

All over the west there are increasing water quality problems. Many of the west's wildlife refuges are, like Kesterson, afterthoughts of Bureau of Reclamation water projects and subject first to the demands of agriculture. Many are thus used as sinks for agricultural waste water, and are, in the words of one refuge manager, "at the garbage end of this thing." Reporters from the *Sacramento Bee* found selenium contamination in wildlife refuges in Idaho, Utah, Montana, New Mexico, and Arizona. Federal studies show high arsenic and selenium levels at Stillwater Wildlife Management Area, and high mercury, chromium, and cadmium levels in others. At New Mexico's Bosque del Apache Refuge, wintering grounds for sandhill and whooping cranes, 80 percent of the water is agricultural drainage. Sewage, pesticides, and

industrial wastes from Mexico form suds on the surface of the New River, the chief source of fresh water to the Salton Sea National Wildlife Refuge. Selenium enters San Francisco Bay from oil refineries and print and dye plants. It is thought to afflict clams, dungeness crabs, striped bass, and even waterfowl. In Wyoming, Lockman says, "We average one oil spill into rivers a year." The Riverton Irrigation Project brings such high levels of chemical fertilizer into Utah's Ocean Lake Waterfowl Management Area that dissolved oxygen available to fish is reduced. In Washington, the Columbia River yields fish with high levels of PCBs, and studies show the PCBs are already contributing to reproductive failure in ospreys along the lower part of the river.

All over the west there is the same depressing picture of decreased funding for management of wetland areas. Arizona manages 2.5 million hectares of land for waterfowl in fifteen management areas, but almost all are without permanent staff. State funding for them is about half what it was in 1970. The state abandoned three waterfowl management areas for lack of water. Another was made part of the Cibola National Wildlife Refuge as mitigation for stream channelization, a bureaucratic shuffling that increased wetland habitat on paper without adding an inch on the ground.

In Washington, budget cuts have left staff intact but eliminated funds needed to administer 250,000 acres of wetlands. On the Skagit Waterfowl Management Area, managers plant less grain to feed wintering flocks. The state gave the 10,000-acre McNary Waterfowl Management Area back to the U.S. Army Corps of Engineers because it lacked funds to run it. The engineers had originally given it to the state in mitigation for the loss of wetlands during the construction of McNary Dam. In one Columbia Basin management area, the state owns a tractor but can't afford a driver for it.

Utah can't find funds to get the U.S. Fish and Wildlife Service's National Wetlands Inventory maps completed for the state. Washington can't find funds to hire people to read Landsat photographs in an effort to inventory its wetlands. No state has funds to map its wetlands as a way of trying to inform devel-

Greater yellowlegs, Flathead River Valley, Montana

Snow geese, Tule Lake, Klamath Basin, California

Silver Creek, Idaho

American badger, Malheur Basin, Oregon

Redhead, Ruby Marsh, Nevada

Península de Quevedo, Dimas, Sinaloa, Mexico

Black Turnstones, Yukon-Kuskokwim Delta, Alaska

Snow geese, Tule Lake, Klamath Basin, California

Red-necked grebes, Rocky Mountain Trench, Columbia River, British Columbia, Canada

6 SAVING THE PIECES

Thirty years ago, after a career teaching in southern California, Althea Pratt Broome settled into a 100-year-old farmhouse in Tualatin, Oregon, far from the noise and haste of the city. Althea is a small, determined lady, with watery blue eyes and a deliberate calm. What appealed to her was the quiet, the creek flowing across the farm, and the way the farmhouse fit the rain and the fir trees. She did not plow the fields. A beaver moved in and built a dam on the creek. "As I didn't dredge out down here," she says, "the water began to spread. Pretty soon, I was getting ducks." After a few years, the geese flying south paid calls. One year, one of the geese stayed over the winter, while the rest of the flock went south to the refuges of the Willamette Valley. "He lived with the cow. Every time I brought the cow in to be milked, the goose would stand around and just holler." In spring, the goose flew north with the flock. "But next fall, when the geese came through," she recalls, "one went over and sat down with the cow."

It was exactly the contact with the wider world that Broome sought in buying the farm. Here, she was part of the wind, the water, the tilt of the earth, privy to secrets that came on the wing from the Arctic. It was a life of quiet events, free from the shrillness, glare, and jostling of southern California. But it wasn't easy to maintain. Early on, a neighboring farmer appeared with an armload of dynamite, bent on blowing up the beaver dam. He felt the marsh that was backing up on her farm was threatening. She stood her ground in front of him. " I said, 'You're going to have to blow me up with it.'"

Althea and her husband, Jack, have dug new ponds to spread more water, turning the farm into what is now Hedges Marsh. But events around them have continually made it hard to protect their re-emergent wetland. Tualatin has grown and suburbanized. Roads, houses, and light industry have encroached on the edges of the marsh. Althea and Jack gathered neighborhood support, went to the city, and got it to create a special wetlands protection zone for their farm, perhaps the only wetlands zoning ordinance in the country. They formed a Wetlands Conservancy to develop a constituency for Hedges Marsh and other wetlands around the state. Still, development of adjoining lands could alter Hedges Marsh's water regime. Crowding houses and industry have already driven off the geese. And electroplating shops, auto repair shops, and other small businesses that fringe the marsh now dump toxic chemicals, wittingly and unwittingly, into the water. It's an uphill battle.

Wetland conservationists like the Broomes have had a harder time than, say, river conservationists or coastal zone defenders or advocates of particular forests. They have had deeper prejudices to overcome. Wetlands have been traditionally regarded in the U.S. as waste places, productive of malaria and snakes, rather than of wildlife and clean water. In 1849, 1850, and 1860, Congress gave to fifteen states sixty-five million acres of what it viewed as "swamp lands," urging the states to sell and develop them. In 1876, the president of the American Public Health Association declared, "The state cannot afford to be indifferent to" the presence of swamps "because they check production, limit population and reduce the standard of health and vigor." Between 1940 and 1980, the U.S. Department of Agriculture subsidized the drainage of nearly sixty million acres for farmlands. In the 1950s, promoters selling Florida swamplands for their development potential were regarded as swindlers. Even today, says Wolf Bauer, a Seattle hydrogeologist, "If you want to find the water table, look for a trailer park."

Not until the 1930s were there efforts to save wetlands, and those came chiefly as efforts to save ducks for hunters. During the drought of the 1930s, the duck populations of North America collapsed. The drought that had brought the dustbowl had, in the words of Jay ("Ding") Darling, "blown the wild duck population of North America to an all-time low. Even the ubiquitous mallard were disappearing. By

Snow geese, Tule Lake, Klamath Basin, California

summer, everywhere one went among the old crad-
ling duck marshes and dried up sloughs, the dry and
cracked mud bottoms were splotched with thousands
of clusters of little yellow legs, and here and there a
few wisps of fuzzy down clinging to the immature
skeletons fluttered in the hot winds." Game managers
saw that simply enacting hunting-season and bag
limits wasn't going to conserve waterfowl. What
wildlife needed was habitat.

In 1929, the Migratory Bird Conservation Act authorized purchase of lands as refuges for migratory
birds. But there was no funding. Not until 1934—
when Congress passed the Duck Stamp Act, which
required hunters to buy a duck stamp, and dedicated
the proceeds to the purchase of refuge lands—was
money available. With duck-stamp money, the New
Deal doubled the size of the federal wildlife refuge
system. Today, there are 425 federal wildlife refuges,
encompassing eighty-nine million acres, and three-
fourths of them are set aside primarily for migratory
waterfowl. The states, too, began in the 1930s to set
aside wetlands as waterfowl management areas.

For the next thirty-five years, wetlands conservation remained largely a matter of duck and goose
management. Most of the efforts came from the U.S.
Fish and Wildlife Service and state game agencies. In
1954, the service undertook the first national inventory of wetlands that was not aimed at finding
land to fill. The service estimated that more than
35 percent of the nation's original wetlands had been
drained, and declared, "Never before in the Nation's
history has it been so necessary to plan for the setting
aside of land and water areas to serve the future needs
of fish and wildlife, as well as to provide for the recreational needs of people who depend on these resources." Two years later, Congress authorized the
service to purchase conservation easements on private
wetlands, and five years later, Congress passed the
Wetlands Loan Act, authorizing loans from general
funds to be used for wetlands purchases and later paid
back from duck-stamp proceeds. In 1962, Congress
prohibited the Department of Agriculture from paying farmers to drain potholes in Minnesota and the
Dakotas. In 1970, Congress enacted the Water Bank
Program, under which the Department of Agricul-

ture might pay farmers for leaving wetlands wet.
(Less than 4 percent of the expenditures under the
Water Bank Program have been made in the Pacific
flyway, all of them in California.)

Two developments broadened interest in wetlands
in the last two decades. In the early 1970s, coastal
states began to see their coastlines fall to unregulated
development and, spurred by the federal Coastal
Zone Management Act, the states began to plan and
regulate coastal development. The planning process
entailed inventories of coastal wetlands. When the
states saw how rapidly coastal wetlands were disappearing, they enacted regulations to slow the trend.
Today, all the coastal states except Texas have strong
coastal wetland regulations.

And in 1972, the federal Water Pollution Control
Act was amended to require the U.S. Army Corps
of Engineers to regulate the discharge of any dredge
spoils or fill materials into the nation's waterways. The
corps had, under the 1899 Rivers and Harbors Act,
required permits for developments in navigable waterways. Since 1968, the corps had considered fish and
wildlife in the permit process, and, in 1970, the
courts upheld a corps denial of a permit to protect
fish and wildlife. A 1972 amendment broadened the
corps' jurisdiction beyond navigable waters, but the
corps has been reluctant to assume this broader au-
thority. A 1975 court decision, however, directed the
corps to do so, and, in 1986, the Supreme Court
unanimously ruled that the corps had jurisdiction
over wetlands adjacent to navigable waterways. The
Section 404 permits do not apply generally to agricultural activities, which make up more than 80 percent of current wetland conversions, but they clearly
apply to port, housing, and industrial park developments—indeed, to any fill intended to convert a wetland to a new use.

There are state programs aimed at inhibiting wetland conversions. Washington's Shoreline Protection
Act, Oregon's Removal-Fill Law, and California's
Coastal Zone Management Act require special permits for filling coastal marshes and call for mitigation
for most marshlands lost. But, because they encompass more lands, the Fish and Wildlife Service's waterfowl programs and the Army Corps of Engineers'

404 permit program are our principal means of conserving wetlands. And there is considerable dis-
agreement as to whether these two programs are adequate tools.

The Fish and Wildlife Service, for example, is
powerless to stop farmers from draining privately
owned wetlands. Farmers are reluctant, too, to sign
easements binding them to wetlands conservation because such easements limit the land's value when the
farmer goes to get a bank loan. And where lands have
been put into wildlife refuges, they haven't always
been adequate to wildlife's needs. In 1972, Congress
established the San Francisco Bay National Wildlife
Refuge. A plan by the Leslie Salt Company, the
largest landowner on south San Francisco Bay, to
build a new city of 50,000 inhabitants near the eastern
end of Dumbarton Bridge was what mobilized Bay
Area residents to push for the refuge in the first place.
When the refuge was authorized, it took in the lands
slated for development first. The seasonal ponds behind the dikes weren't of as much interest because
they had received little attention from developers.
Says Roger Johnson, manager of the refuge, "When
we were putting together the refuge, we erred in as-
suming that some of the open agricultural land was
going to remain vacant forever and a day." Today,
nearly every vacant acre of land around the refuge is
slated for development, and much of it is habitat the
wildlife of the refuge depends upon.

On a March afternoon in 1986, Lynn Tennefoss of
the Santa Clara Valley Audubon Society stood with
Roger Johnson on a hill behind refuge headquarters,
looking at the neighboring lands. To the south rose a
mountain of salt, evaporated from diked ponds by
the Leslie Salt Company. Near the salt pile is a treeless
stretch of cordgrass and pickleweed, a marsh that
Leslie sold to a developer. The developer claims it is
not a wetland, but a bittern pond—a place into which
Leslie dumped the impurities pumped off the evap-
orating salt—and that the bittern, rather than a natural source of water, is responsible for the aquatic
vegetation. The developer holds that the Corps of
Engineers has no jurisdiction over his plans to fill.

To the south, Tennefoss points out Whistling
Wings, a patch of deep-green salt grass edging out

Tule Geese, Sutter Buttes, Sacramento Valley, California

into a slough. There are ducks floating on the slough and egrets flying over the marsh. Whistling Wings takes its name from a duck hunting club that operated there for decades. A developer bought the land and evicted the hunters. The club, maintaining that it still had a lease on the land, called the corps to determine wetlands jurisdiction. By the time the corps got around to it, the developer had taken down a levee and was discing under the alkali bullrush. Next to Whistling Wings is a 300-acre plot that shows up a lighter yellow-green. For seventy years, that tract was an active duck club. The developer now maintains it is not a wetland. He lowered a tide gate, drained the marsh, then leveled the land. He tried seeding it with grasses that didn't survive, then managed to get barley to grow over the *Salicornia.* Clearly, he means to get the corps to identify it as a farm. But for the time being, he refuses to let corps inspectors enter the property to determine whether it is a wetland.

Looking east, there are two disced fields below the refuge overlook, plots which have been drained and leveled. Beyond them is Mayhew's Landing, a wetland on which a developer hoped to raise a golf course and a housing development. Where hills rise, there is the familiar soft green of a golf course. But in low places are patches of coyote brush and other weeds, suggesting water in the soil. The present owner wants to put more dirt on it and replant it. In its original determination, the corps could find only fifteen acres of wetland on the tract. The Fish and Wildlife Service felt there were three times that. In 1985, the developer put tractors on the land to disc the uplands. He had agreed to leave the wetlands alone, but refused to let refuge officials stake out the boundaries between uplands and wetlands. The tractor drivers disced into the wetlands. An alert neighbor called the corps, the Fish and Wildlife Service, the EPA, local conservationists, and news reporters, who all came out and caught the developer in the midst of an illegal fill.

North of the refuge is Ponderosa, a tract which also hosted duck clubs. The developer evicted the duck clubs, flattened the levees, and installed pipes to transport surface water to underground aquifers. The land has been disced so often that the aquatic vegetation is gone and weedy *Rumex,* cockleburs, and wild radishes grow on it. The corps ruled the land wasn't a wetland because it had no historic connection to tidal areas. Because the corps declined jurisdiction, the Fish and Wildlife Service had no opportunity to point out that the plot was habitat for the endangered salt marsh harvest mouse. Unless it caught the developer running over a mouse, the Fish and Wildlife Service couldn't invoke the Endangered Species Act, but the developer wouldn't let service officials on the land to witness the discing. When the Fish and Wildlife Service showed the corps that the land had once been connected to the bay and that someone long ago had installed a drain, the corps ruled that to stop Ponderosa this late would be a hardship on the developer.

Though the Fish and Wildlife Service opposes any further loss of wetlands in the bay, and the California Department of Fish and Game opposes any wetlands development for projects that aren't water-dependent, neither group can intervene unless the corps accepts jurisdiction and draws the developer into the 404 permit process. Tennefoss believes that despite this handicap the laws made to protect wetlands are adequate if the agencies will simply apply them. "The regulations can be boosted," she says. "But the laws behind them are very good." By repeated calls and meetings with the corps and the Environmental Protection Agency, local conservationists have gotten them to apply those regulations more aggressively. After she and other local conservationists talked with the corps' District Engineer, he went out to look at Mayhews Landing himself, and required a new corps appraisal of the tract that declared that there were forty acres of wetland, not fifteen. And in 1986, bowing to conservationists, the commandant declared that the region would no longer permit developers to use agricultural draining as a ruse to convert land, and that it would prosecute violators if it caught them. "I think it's public concern that moves them," says Tennefoss. "It's both education and pressure. We called them like crazy."

But the corps is by no means committed to wetlands protection. Calvin Fong of the Corps of Engineers says, "The Clean Water Act is not a wetland protection act. It's a water quality act. If Congress wanted it to be a wetlands protection act, they certainly had a lot of opportunity to do it. But Congress did not decide to use the word 'wetlands' in the act itself. Our regulations say we do look at wetlands and give them careful consideration. But there are gaping loopholes in the 404 program. There are all kinds of ways of destroying a wetland other than filling it."

Many conservationists feel the 404 program is woefully inadequate. David Ortman of Friends of the Earth points to a fill in Grays Harbor, Washington, by the ITT Corporation in 1980. At the time, the Environmental Protection Agency, the National Marine Fisheries Service, the state fisheries agency, and the Fish and Wildlife Service all complained that the fill was illegal. Nevertheless, a year later, the corps issued an after-the-fact permit. Says Ortman, "The 404 program says the disposal of dredge and fill material basically shall be done with a permit. That's all the 404 section says. Basically it's talking about getting rid of something. You have waste, where does this stuff go?" Because of this, he says, "I don't think the Clean Water Act is a great saver of wetlands. It gives itself all the discretion to do whatever it wants."

Ralph Rogers, wetland ecologist for the Environmental Protection Agency in Seattle, agrees. "The federal program isn't very good in its present form or its administration," he says. "What we need is a national wetlands program. A wetlands protection law should cover all activities that affect wetlands, the digging of ditches, wholesale draining, the loss of vegetation, anything that degrades a wetland." Ortman would like to see Congress take the 404 program away from the Corps of Engineers and lodge it in a more conservation-minded agency. And while some congressmen have been said to have considered such a move, no alternative national wetlands management policy had emerged by 1986.

So conservationists around San Francisco Bay will have to continue working with the corps. And that is an uncertain technique. For even if the corps were committed to protecting wetlands, the federal attorneys the corps must rely upon to file enforcement suits under Section 404 might be less interested in pursuing an illegal wetland developer than, say, a pornographer or a drug dealer. Eight months after the regional commandant announced that the corps was contemplating suits against several violators on San Francisco Bay, no suits had yet been filed. And the regional command of the corps changes every two years. There is no assurance that the next District En-

Northern pintail, San Francisco Bay, California

Snail kite, Rio Tempisque Basin, Costa Rica

Bald eagle, Bahia Magdalena, Baja California Sur, Mexico

Black brant, Izembek Lagoon, Alaska

Marismas nacionales, Sinaloa/Nayarit, Mexico

Western sandpipers, Copper River Delta, Alaska

Fulvous whistling ducks, Ensenada del Pabellon, Sinaloa, Mexico

Black-bellied whistling ducks, San Blas, Nayarit, Mexico

Blue-winged teal, Rio Tempisque Basin, Costa Rica

Bahia de San Esteban, Topolobampo, Sinaloa, Mexico

Black-bellied whistling ducks, Navojoa, Sonora, Mexico

Jabiru, Rio Tempisque Basin, Costa Rica

Magnificent frigatebirds & marbled godwits, Bahia Magdalena, Baja California, Mexico

Most of the people I have met who worry about the fate of wetlands are people who grew up in areas where there were marshes and tide flats and bottom lands and saw them diked and drained and buried beneath tractor wheels, subdivisions, and industrial parks. David Lockman, waterfowl coordinator for Wyoming, grew up hunting and fishing on the South Platte River near Denver. Says Lockman, "All the areas I used to fish and trap have been filled in for intensive subdivisions. It's all gone." Robert Armstrong, a fisheries biologist and wildlife photographer in Juneau, Alaska, worries about plans for development in the nearby Mendenhall Wetlands. "Where I grew up in Tacoma," he says, "I had a favorite swamp that I traipsed in. I knew where every raccoon was, where every trout was. It is now completely paved over, and the site of a shopping center." David Brown, who inventoried Arizona's wetlands, grew up on the shores of San Francisco Bay. They all watched a familiar landscape disappear and felt that an important vision of the world went with it.

They were probably unusual people. While most Americans have at least a nodding acquaintance with mountains and seacoasts, they have lost sight of the wetlands. It is especially so in the coastal cities, where most residents were born into the age of channels and levees. Perhaps that connection with wetlands is inborn, or acquired early in life.

I grew up on the edge of San Francisco Bay. Its sounds have been in my ears, its scents in my nose, for most of my life. Today, watery places tug at my imagination, much the way mountain ranges and seacoasts tug at it. Such places seem mysteriously charged. I cannot drive over a bridge or past a marsh without feeling a kind of beckoning, feeling the pull of the sheen on mud or the glare of sunlight on water. It is the kind of tug I feel when I see the dark blue of a mountain range emerge from distant clouds. The pulse quickens, the eye sharpens, the imagination leaps. I expect to see something significant there, something finely crafted and musical. I have felt the same anticipation on seeing Mount Everest gleaming white out of the Himalayan Range, driving around a bend in the road near Ravallo, Montana, and seeing the molar white of the Mission Range loom out of the east, or looking up through the gunmetal blue haze of the East African plain to see Kilimanjaro hovering above me, as if it floated on air. It is a feeling I cannot experience in the city.

As I drive down a back road in Florida, the glint of water snaps my head around, and I am looking into the knobby eyes of an alligator. The same tug comes from the quiet wake of a merganser swimming on a lily-covered pond in Portland. On a lonely marsh on Utah's Green River, I looked up to see a coyote dashing across the shallows, the splash of his footsteps clearly audible across a quarter of a mile of desert air, the glint of goose behind his eye ringing in my imagination. I watch flocks of marbled godwit feeding on a San Francisco Bay mud flat and feel that this is as significant and as beautiful a part of the earth as Yellowstone's geysers or Maui's beaches. And I feel a sense of connection to the place.

I have seen this sense glowing in the eyes of others. I think of Dan Charles, an old Yupik Eskimo in his fishing camp on the banks of Alaska's Kuskokwim River. The camp is near Bethel, where the tidal bore still lifts the fresh water in the afternoon. Charles is dressed in dirty khaki clothes, a baseball cap on his head. He sits in a wooden chair on the bank of the river, next to racks of bright orange salmon, butterflied and willow-skewered and drying in the summer sun. Charles had suffered a heart attack three days before.

He looked out over the river that flowed by at his feet, and recalled how he had come up it from a coastal village in 1928, a year of poor hunting, to find work so that he could feed his family. He stayed, and the river had given him food—perhaps more than half of what he had eaten in his life, in the form of salmon. It fed his sled dogs and his children. His children were gone now. He no longer kept dogs. He was old, and he was going to die. The heart attack was the knock of fate, and he had not summoned a doctor.

American wigeon, Bolinas Lagoon, California

He stared at the river, drifting with the current and the play of light, and talked of how the river had changed from year to year. He pointed out a spot where, in a dry year, he had walked across the river and water had come only to midcalf. He told how in winter he had run dog sleds over the ice, how in summer he worked his nets and put up fish and got along on three hours of sleep a night. He talked of the salmon that raced, like the thoughts of gods, under the turgid green waters, upstream, every year to spawn in side creeks beyond the tidal bore. He paused and gazed at the river and thought about his life, which had come to a bend, and this river, which had wound through his life. And he grew silent.

It was not a sad moment. You could see in his eyes that he felt the river and his life were of the same breath, that the river would go on, full of gurgle and eddy and the dazzle of sunlight and the deliverance of salmon, down to the sea, where it would spill into the immensity and the eternity of time. And as he talked, I felt he did not look upon death as an ending, but simply as a bend in the river, a turn toward a new angle of descent.

What happens to our sense of time and space when the river no longer runs, when the water is wrung out of the earth, the world stood on its head, the land transformed with human reach and teeming numbers? We talk of the value of lost wetlands in economic terms. We must also talk of values to our hearts and minds.

What is the value, for example, of a vision? Of a pond so still and gray that the only way you can see where the water leaves off and the sky begins is to step into it and look for the ripples. Clouds above, clouds below, silver linings at your feet and birds flying upside down against their own bellies. A bufflehead hen takes off, her wing tips meeting the tops of a mirror image, a duck dancing with a companion that exists only in the medium of light.

On an August evening, I went to watch the sun set on the edge of San Francisco Bay. Near my home is a municipal duck pond, a concrete vessel on the edge of the bay that draws wintering migrants and the Easter ducklings local children have tired of. Just beyond the pond, behind a dike, is a tidal slough on which ruddy ducks, avocets, stilts, and shorebirds of all sizes congregate. The first autumn migrants were coming through, and a flock of western sandpipers settled like windblown leaves over the mud. I sat on the levee between the duck pond and the slough, watching the sun drop behind the heads of godwits and willets. The water rippled gently in grays and purples, muddy echoes of the pastel pinks of a wetland sunset. The shorebirds stood quietly, as if they, too, were absorbed in the color. I sat for fifteen minutes.

I heard a muttering at my feet. Two mallards were waddling past, from pond to slough, inches away, apparently blind to my presence. There was more muttering. I turned my head slowly toward the pond. Several hundred ducks had gathered at the edge of the pond and were getting out, in ones and twos, and marching in a line past me from pond to slough. Almost all the wild ducks on the pond joined in this tiny migration. In the deepening gloam of dusk, they seemed to have some errand on the slough. And they seemed unafraid of me. A few stopped and looked up as they passed, hesitated, backed off, and muttered. But others pushed by, and the timid birds scurried past, giving me worried sidelong glances. They padded down the mud flat and into the slough—a ribbon of ducks several hundred yards long—and swam quietly into the night.

I do not know what this parade was about. But I suggest that for all a duck's strangeness, there is something knowing in its amber eye. It is not a calculated knowledge, but something seated deeper, at the back of its nose or the bottom of its heart. Ungainly as a duck is on land, rumpled as the quack of a mallard is, ducks are not comical. In the air, they are willed and graceful. A duck must be allowed at least the intelligence to get from Canada to Mexico without getting lost. A duck knows, when hunters are afield, to hole up in a refuge sanctuary and feed by night. It wouldn't surprise me, someday, to find some researcher demonstrating that ducks have coherent thoughts and are capable of gossip, sarcasm, and hope.

If the parade is a riddle, watching it reminds me that looking is one of life's great pleasures. To be aware of the light and line and color around you, to look long and thoughtfully at something, to read in a shorebird's plumage the marks of wind and water and time, is one of humankind's gifts. Simply being in a wetland offers us vast opportunities to see.

Losing wetlands is, in part, losing the ability to look at things, to see their light and mass, color and edge. City life closes our eyes to such things. The city offers many choices to our pocketbooks, but fewer and fewer to our hearts and eyes. We use our eyes on city streets or before television screens, where they turn our dreams into apprehensions of war, panic, mugging, and ruin. What we see increasingly makes us afraid of our imaginations. And as we grow to fear what we imagine, we shrink from dreams. We are threatened with boredom, sameness, perhaps even the death of story and faith. Such things were once nurtured in wetlands. Such things may survive in them.

Brown pelicans, Bahia Magdalena, Baja California Sur, Mexico

Eelgrass beds, Izembek Lagoon, Alaska

White ibis, Rio Tempisque Basin, Costa Rica

Northern sea otters, Izembek Lagoon, Alaska

Grizzly bear & sockeye salmon, Brooks River, Alaska

Mangrove, Canal del Infiernillo, Sonora, Mexico

Cinnamon teal, Navojoa, Sonora, Mexico

Sharp-tailed sandpiper, Izembek Lagoon, Alaska

Ensenada del Pabellon, Sinaloa, Mexico

River otters, Bear River Marsh, Willapa Bay, Washington

Western sandpiper, Copper River Delta, Alaska

Northern pintail, Ensenada del Pabellon, Sinaloa, Mexico

Western sandpipers & dunlin, Copper River Delta, Alaska

Red fox, Izembek Lagoon, Alaska

Willow ptarmigan, Izembek Lagoon, Alaska

Willapa Bay, Washington

Teshekpuk Lake, Alaska

Bahia Kino, Sonora, Mexico

Canvasback ducks, San Francisco Bay, California

Mackenzie Delta, N.W.T., Canada

During the course of this photographic survey, I was impressed by two phenomena. First, the truly international flavor of such an entity as the Pacific flyway. This feeling of being beyond boundaries was brought home to me at different times and at different locations. I watched a shorebird, born in Siberia, pick insects out of a grizzly bear track in an Alaskan mud flat to gain weight for a migration to New Zealand. Standing in a marsh in California's great Central Valley, I saw thousands of pintail ducks from Canada drop out of a sky laced with clouds from a Mexican storm. While drifting off to sleep in my camp next to a Costa Rican river delta, I listened to the contented whistling of blue-winged teal, which I had heard before on the Canadian prairie, mixed with the roaring of howler monkeys and the wail of the laughing falcon.

Second, even though fascinated by wild animals and their habits, I had little or no idea of the far-reaching influences of wetlands and the diversity of life they support. I expected, for example, that the great inland freshwater delta of the Peace-Athabasca rivers would hold ducks—but the annual flooding of this delta creates the largest area of undisturbed grasslands in North America, and I saw that these grasslands also support bison, which in turn feed wolves. I knew that the great river deltas, such as the Mackenzie, that flow into the Arctic Ocean are the summer home of many species of shorebirds, but discovered, too, that the beautiful white whale (the Belukha) also comes to feed in the shallow, warm waters. I had heard of tremendous eelgrass beds—Izembek Lagoon contains the world's largest, which in the fall feeds the entire black brant population before they migrate south—but was surprised to learn that the detritus (debris) of the eelgrass also provides food for crabs and clams, which provide in turn a rich food source for sea otters. I knew also that the rivers and streams of coastal Alaska, so vital for spawning, attract thousands of salmon of several species each summer and fall, but didn't know that great numbers of grizzly bears and bald eagles come as well to feed on the salmon.

The people I met along the way—Eskimo whalers, Indian moose hunters, Albertan wheat farmers, Washington oystermen, Mexican shrimpers and Costa Rican vaqueros—were as diverse as the wetlands they live upon, but had this in common: the wetlands gave them life. These users know the value, but not the limits, of wetlands. With the scientific savvy of the U.S. Fish and Wildlife Service and the Canadian Wildlife Service and with the insight of the Nature Conservancy, the National Audubon Society, and Ducks Unlimited, the delicate wetlands of the Pacific flyway should remain forever.

Tupper Ansel Blake
Inverness, California

INDEX

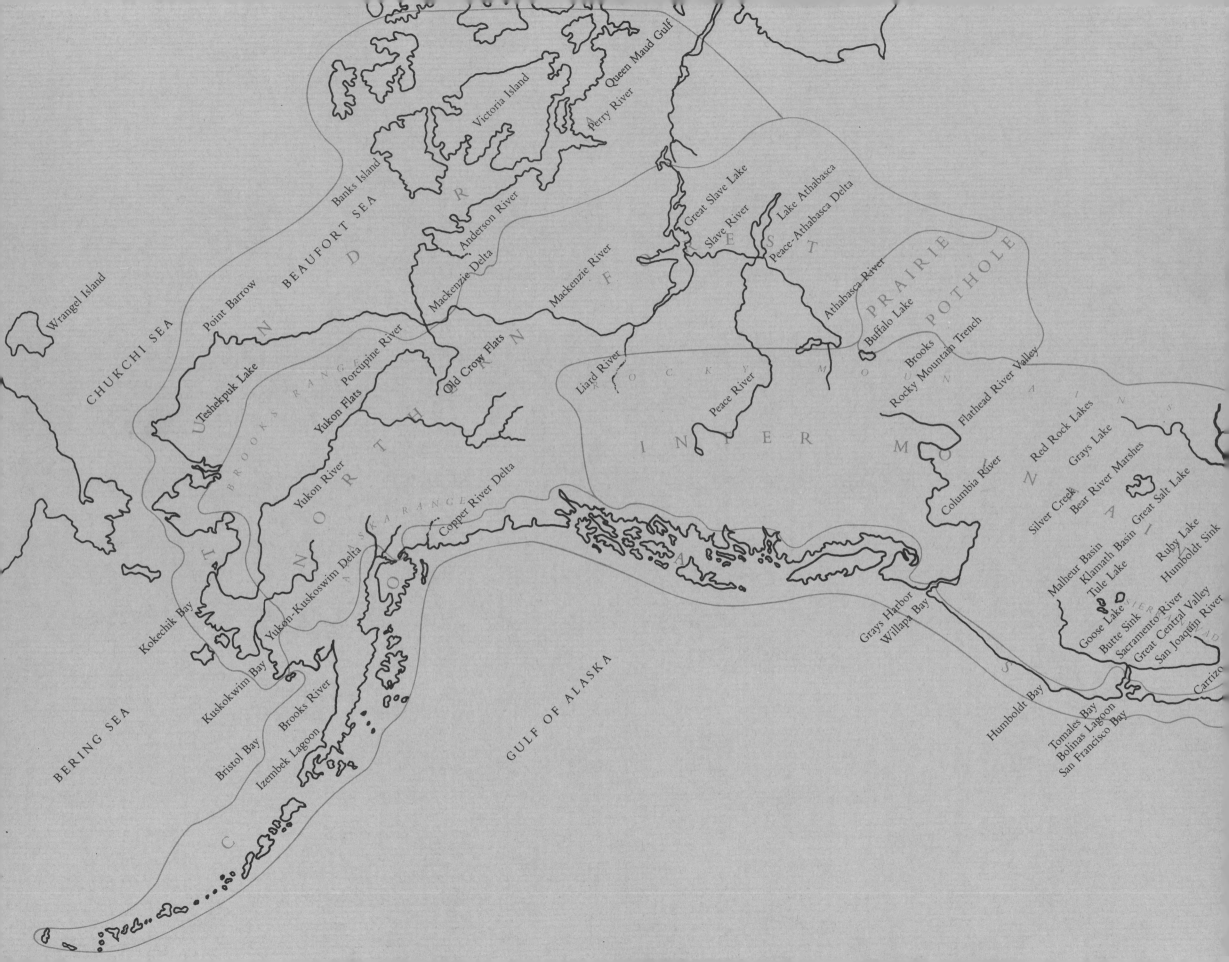